Derrida, Deconstruction and Educati

Derrida, Deconstruction and Education

Ethics of Pedagogy and Research

Edited by
Peter Pericles Trifonas and Michael A. Peters

Blackwell
Publishing

© 2004 by Philosophy of Education Society of Australasia

First published as a special issue of *Educational Philosophy and Theory*, 2003

350 Main Street, Malden, MA 02148-5018, USA
108 Cowley Road, Oxford OX4 1JF, UK
550 Swanston Street, Carlton, Victoria 3053, Australia

First published 2004 by Blackwell Publishing Ltd

Library of Congress Cataloging-in-Publication Data has been applied for

ISBN 1-4051-1953-5

A catalogue record for this title is available from the British Library.

Set by Graphicraft Typesetters Limited, Hong Kong
Printed and bound in the United Kingdom
by MPG Books Ltd, Bodmin, Cornwall

For further information on
Blackwell Publishing, visit our website:
http://www.blackwellpublishing.com

Contents

Notes on Contributors

Patti Lather is a Professor in the Cultural Studies in Education Program, School of Educational Policy and Leadership at Ohio State University, where she teaches qualitative research in education and gender and education. Her work includes *Getting Smart: Feminist research and pedagogy with/in the postmodern* (Routledge, 1991) and, with Chris Smithies, *Troubling the Angels: Women living with* HIV/AIDS (Westview, 1997), which received a Choice Award as one of the best academic books of the year. Recent articles have appeared in *Harvard Educational Review*, 66:3 (1996), *Qualitative Studies in Education*, 13:2 (2000), and *Educational Theory*, 44:4 (1998). She has chapters in the *Handbook of Research on Teaching*, ed. V. Richardson (2001); *Working the Ruins: Feminist Theory and Methods in Education*, ed. E. St. Pierre and W. Pillow (2000), and *The Handbook of Ethnography*, ed. P. Atkinson *et al.* (2001). She is presently working on a manuscript, 'Getting Lost: Feminist Efforts toward a Double(d) Science'. Her favourite academic achievements thus far are a 1995 sabbatical appointment, Humanities Research Institute, University of California-Irvine, seminar on feminist research methodology, and a 1997 visiting appointment at Göteborg University in Sweden.

Denise Egéa-Kuehne is Director of the French Education Project for Research and Teacher Education and Associate Professor, Department of Curriculum and Instruction at Louisiana State University, Baton Rouge. She has been an Invited Scholar at the Institut National de Recherche Pédagogique, Paris, France. Her areas of research center around curriculum theory, philosophy of education, critical theory and cultural studies with a focus on French authors. She lectures and publishes in North America and Europe on issues of diversity, languages, human rights and related ethico-political issues. She recently co-authored and co-edited a book with Gert Biesta, *Derrida & Education* (Routledge). She is currently working on the texts of Levinas, Serres and Derrida.

Peter Pericles Trifonas teaches Social and Cultural Studies in Education at the Ontario Institute for Studies in Education / University of Toronto. His areas of interest include ethics, philosophy of education, cultural studies, and technology. Among his books are the following: *Revolutionary Pedagogies: Cultural politics, instituting education, and the discourse of theory* (Routledge); *The Ethics of Writing: Derrida, deconstruction, and pedagogy* (Rowman & Littlefield); *Ethics, Institutions and The Right to Philosophy* (with Jacques Derrida); *Roland Barthes and the Empire of Signs* (Icon); *Umberto Eco & Football* (Icon); *Pedagogies of Difference* (Routledge).

Marla Morris is an Assistant Professor of Education at Georgia Southern University. She is author of *Curriculum and the Holocaust: Competing sites of memory* *and representation* (Mahwah, NJ: Lawrence Erlbaum and Associates Publishers, 2001). She is Senior Editor of *Difficult Memories: Talk in a (Post) Holocaust era* (New York: Peter Lang, 2002). She is co-editor (along with Mary Aswell Doll and William F. Pinar) of *How We Work* (New York: Peter Lang, 1999); and also (along with Peter Applebaum and John a. Weaver) of *(Post) Modern Science (Education): Propositions and alternative paths* (New York: Peter Lang, 2001). Morris is Editor of *JCT / the Journal of Curriculum Theorizing*, and has written numerous journal articles on curriculum studies and philosophy of education.

Michael A. Peters is Professor of Education at the University of Glasgow (UK) and the University of Auckland (NZ). He is also Adjunct Professor of Communication Studies at the Auckland University of Technology. He has research interests in educational theory and policy, and in contemporary philosophy. He has published over a hundred articles and some twenty books in these fields, including: *Poststructuralism, Marxism and Neoliberalism* (2001); *Nietzsche's Legacy for Education: Past and present values* (2001) (ed. with James Marshall and Paul Smeyers); *Wittgenstein: Philosophy, postmodernism, pedagogy* (1999) with James Marshall; *Poststructuralism, Politics and Education* (1996); *Curriculum in the Postmodern Condition* (2000) (ed.); *Education and the Postmodern Condition* (1995/97) (ed.).

Robert Luke is a Graduate Fellow with the University of Toronto's Knowledge Media Design Institute and a PhD Candidate in the Department of Curriculum Teaching and Learning, University of Toronto. His research interests include Information and Communication Technologies (ICT) and educational technology policy development, ICT access and accessibility, and the move towards digital citizenship and e-government. His dissertation examines Open Source Learning and the design of community-based e-learning programs. Luke's refereed publications cover many areas relating to online learning and the socio-technical nature of the networked society, and have been published in several books and journals such as *Educational Technology & Society* and *Topia: A Canadian Journal of Cultural Studies*.

Jim Garrison is a professor of philosophy of education at Virginia Tech in Blacksburg, Virginia. His research interests center on pragmatism and education. Jim is a past-president of the Philosophy of Education Society. His most recent book is *William James and Education*, co-edited with Ronald L. Podeschi and Eric Bredo (Teachers College Press, 2002).

Preface

At over 70 years Jacques Derrida, a Frenchman of Jewish extraction who was born and grew up in Algeria, is undoubtedly one of the world's most distinguished contemporary philosophers. As the Stanford University website, http://prelectur. stanford.edu/lecturers/derrida/, indicates, his work has been the subject in whole or part of some 400 books and 'In the areas of philosophy and literary criticism alone, Derrida has been cited more than 14,000 times in journal articles over the past 17 years'. This proves that his work is well cited though not necessarily universally acclaimed or appreciated. Both conservatives and members of the radical left have fiercely attacked his work. The former deny he is a philosopher and the latter dismiss his work as frivolous and apolitical.

How does one represent Derrida and his writing? The linguistic notion of representation is central to Derrida's work and to his critique of Western metaphysics. He is suspicious of the view that language represents the world, at least in any straightforward sense. But 'representation' is also important to him as a political principle indicating the ethical and political stakes in presenting an argument or representing a people, a text, an image, or (one's relation to) another thinker—the so-called 'politics of representation'. Not least, the word 'representation' captures his concerns for the genres of autobiography and confession, of philosophy as a certain kind of writing, of the 'personal voice', and of the signature. Derrida is also careful of journalists and tends to refuse most invitations for interviews, especially by the popular press. Paradoxically, *Points ... Interviews, 1974–1994* (Stanford University Press, 1995), a collection, consisting of twenty-three interviews given over the course of the last two decades, provides a good introduction to Derrida (see especially his 'The Work of Intellectuals and the Press').

Perhaps, more than any philosopher before him, and from his earliest beginnings, Jacques Derrida has called attention to the *form* of 'philosophical discourse'—its 'modes of composition, its rhetoric, its metaphors, its language, its fictions', as he says—not in order to assimilate philosophy to literature but rather to recognise the complex links between the two and to investigate the ways in which the institutional authority of academic philosophy, and the autonomy it claims, rests upon a 'disavowal with relation to its own language'. (His doctoral thesis investigated 'The Ideality of the Literary Object'.) The question of philosophical styles, he maintains, is itself a philosophical question.

'Deconstruction', the term most famously associated with Derrida, is a practice of reading and writing, a mode of analysis and criticism that depends deeply upon an interpretation of the question of style. In this, Derrida follows a Nietzschean–Heideggerian line of thought that repudiates Platonism as the source of all metaphysics in the West from St Paul to Kant, Mill and Marx. Where Heidegger still sees in Nietzsche the last strands of an inverted Platonism, tied to the metaphysics of the *will to power*, and pictures himself as the first genuinely *post*-metaphysical thinker, Derrida, in his turn, while acknowledging his debt, detects in Heidegger's notion of Being a residual and nostalgic vestige of metaphysics. He agrees with Heidegger that the most important philosophical task is to break free from the 'logocentrism' of Western philosophy—the self-presence, immediacy and univocity— that clouds our view and manifests its nihilistic impulses in Western culture. And yet 'breaking free' does not mean overcoming metaphysics. Deconstruction substitutes a critical practice focused upon texts for the ineffable or the inexpressible. It does so, not by trying to escape the metaphysical character of language, but by exposing and undermining it: by fixing upon accidental features of the text to subvert its essential message and by playing off its rhetorical elements against its grammatical structure. Heidegger's strategy for getting beyond 'man' will not do the trick: Derrida suggests that 'a change of style' is needed, one which will 'speak several languages and produce several texts at once', as he says in an early essay, 'The Ends of Man' (in *Margins of Philosophy*, 1982).

As Peter Trifonas states in his Introduction to this special issue 'Jacques Derrida is indeed a most profound thinker of matters educations'. I was delighted when Peter Trifonas accepted an invitation to edit a special issue on the educational significance of the work of Jacques Derrida. Philosophers of education have only recently begun to show an interest in Derrida's work. I am thinking in particular of the edited collection *Derrida and Education* (2001) by Gert J. J. Biesta and Denise Egéa-Kuehne in the Routledge International Studies in the Philosophy of Education. Part of the reason for this delay in the appreciation of Derrida's work in education is the still prevalent but now buried positivist and old analytic attitudes to what the Americans call 'French theory' which I have experienced in New Zealand, the US, and the UK. Much of the hostility is defensive and held by those who have not read Derrida but dismiss his work on hearsay based on journalistic accounts of or academic gossip about 'postmodernism' or 'poststructuralism'. The 'Oxford affair', which refers to the occasion when a group of analytic philosophers attempted (unsuccessfully) to intervene in the internal process of granting him an honorary doctorate, is but one demonstration of these attitudes. If these academics are threatened by him and adopt such transparent unscholarly tactics, then he must be finding his mark as a philosopher.

Peter Trifonas recently has published a book with Jacques Derrida entitled *Institutions, Ethics and the Right to Philosophy* and he also edited a collection *Pedagogies of Difference* (RoutledgeFalmer) based centrally on his work. In this issue he has assembled a group of international scholars to discuss Derrida and philosophy of education. The special issue has been in process for a couple of years. I am thankful to Peter Trifonas and his contributors for an excellent issue.

MICHAEL A. PETERS
University of Glasgow

1

INTRODUCTION

Derrida and the Philosophy of Education

PETER TRIFONAS

Institute for Studies in Education / University of Toronto

> Philosophy consists of offering reassurance to children. That is, if one prefers, of taking them out of childhood, of forgetting about the child, or, inversely, but by the same token, of speaking first and foremost *for* that little boy within us, of teaching him to speak—to dialogue—by displacing his fear or his desire.
>
> —Derrida, *Dissemination*[1]

The essays collected in this Special Issue of *Educational Philosophy and Theory* take the premise that Jacques Derrida is indeed a most profound thinker of matters educational. Each scholar addresses in highly provocative and original ways, the 'unconventional' readings of the history of Western metaphysics that deconstruction engenders regarding some of the most basic philosophical questions of teaching and of learning. Michel Foucault and Edward Said have suggested—albeit in derisive ways—that *deconstruction is perhaps nothing else but the elaborate expression of a new didactics, a poststructural pedagogy of the text.*[2] And yet, on the one hand, to say Derrida presents the means to a *'method' of teaching*, and *this only*, would be wrong, for there are no directives to educational practice prescribed, no rules imposed upon the right to a 'freedom-of-thinking' or responsivity, and no *apriority* of absolute truths to be found as could suffice to constitute the operational basis of an *ideal model or mode of instruction*. But, on the other hand, the *'philosophemes of deconstruction'* carry on the 'contradictory and conflictual' *polemos* of a theoretical backdrop that looks forward to the real necessity of informed action transcribed across the poststructural, post-phenomenological passage from 'thetic' to 'a-thetic' rationality. The 'movement' of deconstruction is away from an obstinate stance of single-minded opposition ready to tear down the existing 'System' and toward an economy of reflective matriculation within the structurality of the institution to a *working-out of the essential trials of its undecidability at the expense of the metaphysical grounding of its architectonics*. Due to the awareness of the stretched parameters of the dilemma of this 'double-sided' strategem—the tensions of its *aporias*—open up the *ethics of deconstruction* with respect to the *politics of education* and there is no need to enact the finality of *the last word* on the subject, especially in the form of a statement, 'of positional or oppositional logic, [overdetermined in] the idea of position, of *Setzung* or *Stellung*' (Derrida, 1983, p. 42). This would be both problematic and irresponsible given the non-adequation of the 'critical demonstra-tivity' of Derrida's texts with the desire for settling upon an undisputable and self-revealing truth. The metaphysico-theoretical fidelity of such a standard closing of argumentation seeking to culminate in a full stop of studied silence would most surely contravene the unpredictable inter-spaces of the *risk of writing* that opens signification up to an in-sertion of the alterity of the Other and invites the creation of the *difference of meaning* as the disseminative interruption of a stable conditionality of the sign. There is thereby a cancelling-out, in advance, of the possibility of any *coming-to-resistance* an examination of the ethico-political exigencies of deconstruc-tion could run against in relation to a 'thinking-of-the-end' as the *telos* of philosophy by being contrapuntal to the *curricularisation of pedagogy* oriented from the 'historico-topologico-socio-cultural' regulation of its implementational styles. Still, we must proffer reasons, and bestow 'sound reasons' in *good faith* for the sake of the insti-tutional reason of deconstruction as a just way of thinking and knowing. It is necessary to justify, in principle and by practice, the tendency of a hesitation to *simply conclude* that deconstruction is a 'philosophy of education', 'of teaching and learning', thus accepting responsibility for the lack of *clôture* to those *unread* or *under-read* texts of Derrida's, the 'educational texts', as I have described them, *writings that will always already be open before us.*

Notes

1. Derrida, 1981, p. 122.
2. See Edward Said, 'The Problem of Textuality' (1978, pp. 673–714), and Michel Foucault, *Madness and Civilization* (1965). In an appendix to the 1972 edition (the original was published in the form of a *Thèse d'Etat* in 1961), Foucault responds to what he perceived to be an 'attack' on his work by Derrida in the 'lecture' 'Cogito and the History of Madness' (Derrida, 1978, pp. 31–63) by describing deconstruction as nothing more than a conservative and well-entrenched 'pedagogy of the text'.

References

Derrida, J. (1978) Cogito and the History of Madness, in: *Writing and Difference*, trans. A. Bass (London, Routledge & Kegan Paul).
Derrida, J. (1981) *Dissemination*, trans. B. Johnson (Chicago, University of Chicago Press).
Derrida, J. (1983) The Time of a Thesis: Punctuations, trans. K. McLaughlin, in: A. Montefiore (ed.), *Philosophy in France Today* (Cambridge, Cambridge University Press).
Foucault, M. (1965) *Madness and Civilization: A history of insanity in the age of reason*, trans. R. Howard (New York, Random House).
Said, E. (1978) The Problem of Textuality: Two exemplary positions, *Critical Inquiry*, 4, pp. 673–714.

2

Applied Derrida: (Mis)Reading the work of mourning in educational research

PATTI LATHER
Ohio State University

> The century of 'Marxism' will have been that of the techno-scientific and effective decentering of the earth, of geopolitics, of the *anthropos* in its onto-theological identity or its genetic properties, of the *ego cogito*—and of the very concept of narcissism whose aporias are ... the explicit themes of deconstruction. This trauma is endlessly denied by the very movement through which one tries to cushion it, to assimilate it, to interiorize and incorporate it. In this mourning work in process, in this interminable task, the ghost remains that which gives one the most to think about—and to do. Let us insist and spell things out: to do and to make come about, as well as to let come (about). (Derrida, 1994, p. 98)

This essay began as part of a symposium on Marxism today.[1] It moves through a necessarily guilty reading of the reception of the 'post' in educational research[2] and then turns to its primary interest, the uses of deconstruction in thinking about the improvement of educational policy and practice through research, by way of a focus on reinscribing praxis under conditions of postmodernity.

Whatever the meaning of the 'post' these days, it is pervasive, elusive and marked by a proliferation of conflicting definitions that refuse to settle into meaning. Efforts to accommodate/incorporate the 'post' in educational research have not been easy. In the pages of the *Educational Researcher* alone, McLaren and Farahmandpur (2000) warn against 'the decline of class politics,' textualism, 'toothless liberalism and airbrushed insurgency,' nihilism, localism and relativism, all wrapped up in 'a facile form of culturalism' that paralyzes progressive politics. Constas (1998) offers a typology of the postmodern noteworthy for its use of the very logic that the 'post' sets out to undo (St. Pierre, 2000; Pillow, 2000). Howe contrasts 'postmodernists' and 'transformationists' and worries about 'paradigm cliques' (1998, p. 20).

Harold Bloom (1975) has famously argued that all readings are misreadings, given the weight of perspective on what we see and how we see it. This essay adapts Bloom's thesis to read the space of the range of discussion concerning the 'post' in educational research as symptomatic of the anxieties attendant upon the collapse of foundations and the end of triumphalist versions of science. In order to make the project doable, I concentrate on the reception of Derrida as a 'part-for-whole' or synecdoche for the heterogeneous 'post' of postmodernism, including deconstruction.

My interest is in three gestures of thought at work in the reception of the 'post' in much of educational research in what might be said, at the risk of a proper reading, to lead to a mistaken identity. The three gestures of thought are: 1) charges of nihilism/textualism, 2) conflating ideology critique and deconstruction, and 3) compelling understanding too quickly in terms of the uses of deconstruction in educational research. I conclude with an example of 'applied Derrida' that troubles the concept of praxis in the context of writing a book about women living with HIV/AIDS (Lather & Smithies, 1997).

Nihilism/Nothing Outside the Text

Derrida's 'there is nothing outside the text' from *Of Grammatology* (1976, pp. 226–227) is, according to John Caputo, 'one of the most thoroughly misrepresented utterances in contemporary philosophy' (1997a, p. 78). Rather than some scandal of 'linguisticism' (Derrida, in Caputo 1997a, p. 104), Derrida means by this that there are no cultural practices that are not defined by frameworks that are 'caught up in conflicting networks of power, violence, and domination' (Baker, 1995, p. 129). Derrida says 'I never cease to be surprised by critics who see my work as a declaration that there is nothing beyond language … it is, in fact, saying the exact opposite. The critique of logocentrism is above all else the search for the "other" and the "other of language" … If deconstruction *really* consisted in saying that everything happens in books, it wouldn't deserve *five* minutes of anybody's attention' (quoted in Baker, 1995, p. 16).

Rather than an occlusion of 'the real,' the deconstructive claim is that there is nothing that is not caught in a network of differences and references that give a textual structure to what we can know of the world. There is a 'thereness' that includes the frames, horizons of intelligibility, and sociopolitical presuppositions of the necessary, irreducible and inescapable epistemic and archival violence that constitute Derridean textuality. This is about the loss of transcendental signifiers and the situating of reference within the differential systems from which making meaning is possible. To quote Derrida, 'Deconstruction starts with the deconstruction of logocentrism, and thus to want to confine it to linguistic phenomena is the most suspect of operations' (in Brunette & Wills, 1994, p. 15).

Working the failure of the oppositions that assure concepts, deconstruction remains in excess of traditional political agendas. The speculative force of this excess works toward establishing new relational structures with 'a greater emphasis on ethics and its relationship to the political' (Spivak, 1999, p. 426). 'One needs another language besides that of political liberation,' Derrida says (in Kearney, 1984, p. 122). In deconstruction, the terms of political struggle shift from class as a subject of history to the cultural constitution of subjectivity. Here the complexity of subject formation includes how various axes of power are mutually constitutive, productive of different local regimes of power and knowledge that locate subjects and require complex negotiations of relations, including the interruption of coherence and complete subordination to the demands of regulatory regimes. Engaging the real is not what it used to be. Different ideas about materiality, reality, representations, and truth distinguish different epistemological orientations where reality does not precede representation but is constituted by it. Such a shift from the sociological to the cultural brings textuality, discourse, and representation to the fore. The means of production are less the struggle than 'the nature of social representations' (Foster, quoted in Altieri, 1990, p. 457) with its questions concerning the psyche, subjectivity, and the self as sites of the production of social categories. Calls for 'resistance postmodernism' or 'left deconstruction' à la Tony Bennett and Terry Eagleton, among others, offer a 'reductively oppositional' (Altieri, 1990, p. 475) reading of the post that reinscribes it back into modernist categories of political struggle (e.g. Kincheloe & McLaren, 1994; Gabardi, 2000). Fekete (1992) terms this a recuperation of postmodernism into a politically intelligible place 'in the frame of the already established purposes of the day' on the part of an academic left that earlier dismissed the post.

Derrida is clear that we 'cannot not be' the heirs of Marx's break with myth, religion and nationalism as ways to think the world and our place in it (1994, p. 91). Derrida's 'turn or return to Marx' (p. 32) breaks his silence on Marx in the face of proclamations as to 'the end of Marxism' (p. 32). He seeks the Marx outside of 'the dogma machine' (p. 13) where the place for justice is 'the infinite asymmetry of the relation to the other' (p. 22) as our way into a better future (Spivak, 1994, p. 55). Against charges of the nihilism of deconstruction, Derrida speaks of 'a certain configurativity' where 'the coming of the other' produces a democracy to come (Sprinkler, 1993, p. 231). In a present marked not by crisis so much as by *structural incompetence*, a 'wearing down beyond wear' of the 'conceptual phantasms' that have guided us through modernity (Derrida, 1994, p. 80), Derrida sees a moment of contestatory possibilities where more is at stake than philosophy when philosophy is at stake.

Spivak terms this a place for justice, a problematic of a responsibility, 'caught between an ungraspable call and a setting-to-work' (1994, p. 23). Other to 'inspirational academic heroics' (p. 26), a problematic of responsibility is premised on 'the something that must of necessity not go through' (p. 20). Rather than a task of uncovering hidden forces and material structures and reinscribing a textual(rhetorical)/ real(material) binary and oppositional (dialectical) contradictions, this is about working the ruins of Marxism toward an other logic. As delineated in *Specters of Marx*, this different logic works against the leveling processes of the dialectic and for the excess, the nonrecuperable remainder, the different, the other/outside of the logic of noncontradiction.

Worries about privileging text over people and narrative over life elide how the real is no longer real in a digitalized era that interrupts the easy real (Poster, 1989). How discourse enframes and worlds the world becomes the issue rather than search for the 'beyond' of ideology of 'real' social forces and material structures. Instead of the nihilism so frequently evoked by the educational left in its efforts to make sense of the post, this is the yes of the setting to work mode of deconstruction that faces unanswerable questions, 'the necessary experience of the impossible' in responding to the call of the wholly other (Spivak, 1999, p. 428).

Conflating Ideology Critique and Deconstruction

Understanding the social and historical meanings of representational practices has encountered much resistance from traditional positivist knowledge approaches, but this is a shared project of Marxism and the post. There are, however, key differences between ideology critique and deconstruction.

Ideology critique is about uncovering hidden forces and material structures in a discursive field organized by concerns for 'truth.' It endorses a binary of textual/material in its calls for grounding knowledge in 'the crucial facticity of determinant brute economic reality' (Leslie, 2000, p. 33). An Enlightenment project, a modernist project, it offers a material real in contrast to the ontological uncertainty of deconstruction. 'If such a thing exists,' Derrida writes, over and over again, marking that indeterminacy that is the 'originary complication' of a deconstruction that is not an unmasking but a keeping open, alive, loose, on guard against itself.

The critique of ideology was the 'essence of structuralist cultural studies' in a way that moved from interpreting reality as determined by some assumedly knowable empirical and historical presence to attending to the unconscious, imaginary relations and the construction of subjectivity (Van Loon, 2001, p. 275). Experience became an effect of structure in an early version of the decentering of the subject that prepared the way for the linguistic turn that followed Althusserean structuralist Marxism. From early semiology through discourse analysis to an increasing attention to deconstruction, troubling language as a transparent medium has undercut universal categories and a romanticized, universalized subject.

Deconstructive destabilization works otherwise. Its interest is in complicit practices and excessive differences rather than unveiling structures and illuminating the forces and relations of production. Purposefully doubled in its necessary implications in what it seeks to trouble, deconstruction works against the critical righteousness of ideology critique where 'the materialist critic has an educative role that involves the propagandistic task of eliciting correct consciousness' (Leslie, 2000, p. 33). In reading the subject, modes of investment are no longer based on traditional notions of categorical thinking such as false consciousness, on the one hand, or the more idealized model of intentional agency of reason and will. Indeterminacy and paradox become conditions of affirmative power by undoing fixities and mapping new possibilities for playing out relations between identity and difference, margins and centers. Ways of knowing become 'an archive of windows,' a study of the histories of enframing that focuses on the staging of truthfulness. Particularly interested in that which works to efface the frame effect, the deconstructive shift is from the real to the production of the reality effect. In this shift, practices dedicated to the disappearance of anything easily identifiable as 'the real' are claimed as political work.

Practices of respectful twisting open up to difference and get things moving as practical or praxiological engagements that say yes to turning forms against themselves. This is an immanent critique, a critical intimacy of intervention from within as there is no outside. Quite other to the masterful, totalizing critical distance of ideology critique, this is Derrida's thesis of necessary complicity, the necessity of participating in what is being reinscribed in a way that responds to the call of the wholly other. Perplexed by design, doubled in implication, the practical politics of putting deconstruction to work entail a sort of getting lost as an ethical relationality of non-authoritarian authority to what we know and how we know it.

Applied Post: Misreading the work of mourning

In an interview for the 1995 conference, 'Applying: To Derrida,' Derrida says, 'Deconstruction cannot be applied and cannot not be applied. So we have to deal with this aporia, and this is what deconstruction is about,' (1996, p. 218). In order to invent the impossible, application is much more about dissemination and proliferation under conditions of responsibility within indeterminacy, 'a moment of non-knowledge, a moment beyond the programme' (p. 223) than it is about something technical and neutral, programmable and predictable.

Calls to attend to the real world, 'a mobilization of a sense of urgency—an urgency to act, to declare, to represent, to render an account,' are situated in the history of the fraught relationship between French and continental philosophy and Anglo-Saxon sociohistorical empiricism (Van Loon, 2001, p. 280). Against the 'fiddling while Rome burns' characterizations of deconstruction, deconstruction is aimed at provoking fields into new moves and spaces where they hardly recognize themselves in becoming otherwise, the unforeseeable that they are already becoming. Any demand that it serve an immediate and evidently useful purpose belies its 'exorbitant method' that is loyal to a tradition by keeping it alive while transgressing the horizon of legitimation, a performative within/against where it is what it does in an undecidability that is never done with (Caputo, 1997a, 1997b).

One could talk of a 'public or perish' governing mentality of educational research of late, the increased demand for its usefulness in the context of policy and practice (Willinsky, 2001). It is tempting to revert to the quick and narrow scientism of the past. But the game has changed. Accounting for complexity and contingency without predictability is what now shapes our conversations and expands our idea of science as cultural practice and practice of culture. My argument is that cutting-edge educational research will be produced out of and because of the paradoxes of projects that develop a better language to describe a more complicated understanding of what knowledge means and does than by reinscribing the idealized natural science model.[3]

Make something new, Derrida says, that is how deconstruction happens. In the final section of this essay, putting deconstruction to work, I use the efforts of my co-researcher, Chris Smithies, and myself to tell the stories of women living with HIV/AIDS to ask hard questions about necessary complicities, inadequate categories, dispersing rather than capturing meanings, and producing bafflements rather than solutions. As what Spivak calls 'a practical academic' (1994, p. 27), I will draw on this work not so much to give flesh and blood to abstractions as to evoke what Derrida terms a 'ghost effect' of spectral movement where ontology can only be a conjuration, a more demanding ontology of an other logic calling for other concepts.

In *Specters of Marx*, exploring a logic of mourning and haunting, Derrida enacts an inbetween logic, between presence and absence, in order to unlock thinking and help us otherwise. What I have discovered in my reading of this book is that my mourning in relation to Marxism is for a certain praxis characterized by salvation narratives, consciousness-raising, and a romance of the humanist subject and agency. In spite of poststructural critiques of the doctrine of eventual salvation, voluntaristic philosophies of consciousness and vanguard theories of 'emancipating' some others implicit in Marxism, I am unable to do without the concept of praxis. It seems to be the space, for me, of the 'experience of the promise' of Marxism.

In the distinctions Krell (2000) draws between Freud and Derrida, it is impossible mourning, unsuccessful mourning that is, in Derrida, the very promise of affirmation. As opposed to Freud's theorized 'hyperbolic identifications and narcissistic or anaclitic object choices in the first place' (p. 15), Krell sees the undecidability of Derrida's mourning as facing that 'there never was any *there* there for us' (p. 18). Remaining true to the memory of the other is not about withdrawing affirmation but about being 'always a bit lost' (p. 20) to one another, a loss of presence at the heart of being, as opposed to the 'too solidly *taken over*' of the orthodox 'legitimation by way of Marx' (Derrida, 1994, p. 92).

Mourning work always follows a trauma. Philosophically, the work of mourning is about ontologizing what remains after the rigor of troubling or problematizing a concept.

My work in this final section is to use my continued post-Marxist haunting by the ghost of praxis to reinscribe praxis in a way that mourns its remainders and irremediable losses. To be post-Marxist is not so much to be out of date or surpassed as confronted with undecidability, incompleteness and dispersion rather than the comforts of transformation and closure. This calls for a praxis 'after the trial of undecidability,' a praxis of aporia: 'as tentative, contextual, appropriative, interventionist, and unfinished effort to shift the terrain' (Rooney, 1995, p. 195).[4]

Such a move is in, with, for and against the much that must be refused: the privileging of containment over excess, thought over affect, structure over speed, linear causality over complexity, and intention over aggregative capacities (Levinson, 1995). Ontological changes and category slippages mark the exhaustion of received categories of mind/body, nature/culture, organism/machine (Haraway, 1997). The goal is to shape our practice to a future that must remain to come, in excess of our codes but, still, always already: forces already active in the present. Perhaps a transvaluation of praxis means to find ways to participate in the struggle of these forces as we move toward a future which is unforseeable from the perspective of what is given or even conceivable within our present conceptual frameworks.

Praxis Under Erasure: Between concepts

Classically, praxis is the self-creative activity through which we make the world, *the* central concept of a Marxist philosophy that did not want to remain a philosophy, philosophy becoming practical (Bottomore, 1983, p. 386). For the Greeks, *praxis* was the realm of free action of citizens (free men), as distinct from *poiesis*, the servile action of necessity. Marx put together a practice of material transformation that brought these together in a relationship of reciprocity with a theorizing quite other to contemplation, 'proposing to philosophy that it view itself in the mirror of practice' (Balibar, 1995, p. 41).

The concept of praxis has long given me much to think about and to do. My earlier articulation of 'research as praxis' (Lather, 1986) sought that intersection of material transformation through theory's practice and practice's theory. Reprinted in *Getting Smart* (1991), the chapter on research as praxis is the most cited part of the book, even though I now see it as full of unproblematized assumptions about the role of 'transformative intellectuals,' ideology critique, a voluntarist philosophy of consciousness and pretensions toward 'emancipating' or 'empowering' some others. The failure of most readers to trouble the foundationalism of my concept of 'research as praxis' speaks, I think, to the yearning and unsettlement of the academic left, given the demise of humanism and regimes of transcendent generality.

Yearning and unsettled myself, my present reach is toward a praxis thought against the humanist figure of a consciously choosing subject, what Judith Butler refers to as 'a fiction of the ego as master of circumstances' (1993, p. 124). I reach also toward what William Spanos (1993) writes of as the 'postmodern theoretical demystification of the discourse of deliverance' (p. 187) that positions narratives of salvage and redemptive agendas as ever deeper places for privilege to hide. Much of this is prefigured in feminist concerns with emancipatory agendas as under suspicion for their coercion, rationalism and universalism,[5] but deconstruction adds a twist with its central thesis of complicity, its refusal of an innocent position 'outside' power networks. Spivak, for example, claims that 'deconstruction does not aim at praxis or theoretical practice but lives in the persistent crisis or unease of the moment of techne or crafting ... It is a negotiation and an acknowledgement of complicity' (1993, p. 121). Rather than trying to legitimate, a deconstructive problematic tries to trouble, to look for dangers, normalizing tendencies, tendencies toward dominance in spite of liberatory intentions (Sawiki, 1988, p. 166).

What does this mean for the concept of praxis? Has what Gramsci (1971) termed 'the philosophy of praxis' disappeared or is 'the disappeared'[6] the consolations of humanism given the proliferation of differences that signals the radical impossibility of social totalities? To address these questions, I call on Derrida's practice of sous rature or writing under erasure: keeping something visible but crossed out, to avoid universalizing or monumentalizing it, a form of a warning of an irreducibility outside of intentional control in the play of the world, keeping a term as both limit and resource, opening it up to margins. What would be the parameters of a praxis under erasure?

Literary critic, Wlad Godzich postulates that post-Hegelian praxis is about gaps, remains, radical alterities (1994, p. 26), the philosophy of the cry versus the Hegelian philosophy of the concept. Beyond absorption into present frames of intelligibility, such praxis is excessive, diffuse, an exacerbation of the tensions native to concepts that reveals their undecidability, their constitutive exclusions. This sort of category shake-down is evident in Bill Haver's (1996) proposal that the question of how to intervene be grounded in a shift from totalities to non-containment, a principle of excess and infinite proliferation where a rigorous praxis refuses much in an effort to 'stop thinking straight.' Arguing the limits of our frames of intelligibility which render the world thinkable and knowable, Haver moves toward practices that are in excess of subjects presumed to know about objects presumed to be knowable.

Hence what I am trying to think here is a praxis of the trial of undecidability. In excess of binary or dialectical logic, I seek a form of praxis that disrupts the horizon of an already prescribed intelligibility to address Derrida's question: 'What must now be thought and thought otherwise?' (1994, p. 59) The logic of negation as a trial to go through before restoration of some lost unity breaks down in the face of the challenges of social changes which collapse our categories. Derrida (1994) begins a list: labor, production, unemployment, free market, foreign debt, arms industry, inter-ethnic wars, mafia and drug cartels. All present concepts outdated in their very axiomatics by tele-technic dis-location, rhizomatic spreading and acceleration, and new experiences of frontier and identity. In short, the organization of knowledge ruled by the Hegelian inheritance is radically insufficient in the face of a new set of givens that disrupts the conceptual oppositions that structure traditional thinking.

In the post-Enlightenment stirrings and strivings of contemporary theory, the philosophy of the subject, reflection, and praxis are being rethought. Levinson (1995), for example, formulates a 'post-dialectical praxis' that is quite different from a Kantian or Hegelian analytic. The modernist metaphysics of presence, assured interiority and subject centered agency, the valorizing of transformative interest in the object, Hegel's affirmative negativity and dialectical overcoming: all are at risk, refused in a way that attempts to signal the size and complexity of the changes involved. Such a praxis is about ontological stammering, concepts with a lower ontological weight, a praxis without guaranteed subjects or objects, oriented toward the as yet incompletely thinkable conditions and potentials of given arrangements (Levinson, 1995). To explore such a concept of praxis, I turn to Chris and my textual practices in *Troubling the Angels: Women Living With HIV/AIDS*.

X **Caught Between an Ungraspable Call and a Setting-to-Work: Praxis as a living on**

> One makes oneself accountable by an engagement that selects, interprets, and orients. In a practical and performative manner, and by a decision that begins by getting caught up, like a responsibility, in the snares of an injunction that is already multiple, heterogeneous, contradictory, divided. (Derrida, 1994, p. 93)

While Marx questioned the concept, Derrida's interest is 'the concept of the concept' (1994, p. 147), a thinking of excess and dissemination against the limiting fixity of conceptualization. To think praxis as a concept of living on where 'one must work—practically, actually' (p. 131) while, simultaneously, dislocating the self-presence of the concept as a sort of redemption: this is the logic I am trying to enact. Situating praxis as a ruin made habitable by a fold of the between of presence and absence (p. 187), Chris and my practices in *Troubling the Angels* are both more and other than an example. As a topology for new tasks toward other places of thinking and putting to work, I wrestle with what I have learned from our construction of this text of responsibility. My interest is a praxis that attends to poststructuralist suspicions of rationality, philosophies of presence and universalizing projects, a praxis that 'does not put itself in place of theory; it would be theory itself becoming practical—the opposite of pragmatism' (Tiedemann, 1989, p. 202). In terms of *Troubling the Angels*, what did Chris and I do to make (and let) come about in terms of a thinking that comes from practice?

Any research is concrete and complex, a knotted and undecidable situation. Invited in to do the job of getting into general circulation the women's stories of living with HIV/AIDS, Chris and I stumbled into a hypertextual pastiche of split text, angel inter-chapters, and the juxtaposition of various presentations of information, from graphs and charts of demographic variables to participant narratives. Getting lost was one of my methodological goals in my desire to interrupt the reductiveness of restricted economies of representation.[7] Hence *Troubling the Angels* is organized around and courting of complexities and undecidables.

In making textual decisions, Walter Benjamin served as 'an indispensable point of departure' (Holland, 1993, p. 3) in moving toward mosaic, multi-leveled forms of representation. Via a community of quotations, didactics, reflections and images, we intended some clustering that sets up resonances to move readers toward thinking about meaning in history within the crisis of representation. Attempting practices that foster a grasp of the ever-changing logic of the time in which we find ourselves, in this case, of AIDS as a 'massive readability' (Derrida, 1993), our effort was toward reading out traces not only of the history of AIDS but also of history itself, of how history happens. Following Benjamin's textual practice of an assemblage of fragments, a methodical, continuous experiment of conjunction, we jammed ideas, texts, traditions and procedures together. Moving among different levels, our practice condenses and juxtaposes 'different dimensions, of different registers of space and time, of different levels of existence and experience' (Felman & Laub, 1992, p. 262) of a testimony we might prefer not to hear. Facing our own avoidance, we move away from the Marxist dream of 'cure, salvation and redemption' (p. 177) and toward our vacillation between knowing and not knowing. Our questions become, 'What does it mean to inhabit history as crime, as the space of the annihilation of the Other?' (p. 189) What does it mean to be wretched away from received categories of thought, to acknowledge one's intellectual bewilderment, one's noninnocence in the face of the failure of representation? How can articulating the very inarticulateness of history as a limit-experience performatively create in us the power of a call, 'the chance, of our response-ability' (p. 203)? My hope was that the women would react to the book like Derrida did to Geoff Bennington's (1991) writing about him in a split text format where the bottom of each page is Derrida's running commentary, designed to escape, to surprise, the systematization of his work proposed by Bennington in the top page. Bennington refers to the 'hypertext' dimensions of the text that open it to multiple paths of reading (p. 14). Derrida writes of 'what is written "up" there, beside or above me, on me, but also for me, in my favor, toward me and in my place' (p. 26).

The Epilogue of *Troubling the Angels* presents the women's reactions to our writing of their lives and it seems we managed, although unevenly, to satisfy their desire to have their stories out and available to a reading public well beyond the academy. Key here was positioning the women not as objects of exchange and spectacle, voyeurs or eavesdroppers on a conversation not meant for them, but rather as interlocutors of our storying of their lives. Chris called them our editorial board. This destabilized our authorial position and disturbed us by situating them not so much as 'ours' in some possessive prerogative as us 'theirs,' those to whom we were accountable, 'my personal psychologist' as CR referred to Chris, capable of getting 'so much smarter' as Amber referred to me.

Whatever our authorial intentions, we were, as writers, also a registering apparatus, a kind of seismograph, an ensemble, an aggregate of registrations (Holland, 1993, p. 260). Here, quite open to chance, many of which align or resonate with one another, connections are made under contingent circumstances. 'What matters is the registration of historical process, and questions as to the degree of consciousness or unconsciousness of an author simply do not arise' (p. 262). Judith Butler (1993, p. 266), too, speaks of a writing 'which precedes and mobilizes the one who writes, connecting the one who writes with a language which "writes" the one.' Chris and I both knew and did not know what we were doing, both intentional agents and vessels of history writing us in ways we did not and do not always understand.

In sum, given that praxis is a concept I cannot seem to do without, the praxis that I want to salvage from Marxism is a praxis with less ontological content, an immanent praxis of conjunction that calls out aggregative capacities from within the play of the forces of history. The task becomes not so much to invent or incite as to use praxis as a material force to identify and amplify what is already begun (Balibar, 1995, p. 122). In the case of *Troubling the Angels*, to argue for textuality as praxis is a refusal of a textual/material binary toward a practice of living on. This is a non-reductive praxis that calls out a promise, not of a new concept but of practice on a shifting ground that foregrounds the limits of the fixing, locating, defining and confining that is the work of the concept. This is a praxis that can survive the critique of Marxism, a praxis immanent in practices that helps us think not only *with* but *in* our actions.

Conclusion

—Can one ever accept working for His Highness Mourning?—How can one not accept it? That is what mourning is, the history of its refusal, the narrative of your revolution, our rebellion, my angel. (Derrida, 1991, p. 55)

In this essay, I have risked a 'proper reading' of Derrida as endlessly open, enacting a principle of multiplication and dispersion that is neither straightforward continuity nor radical rupture. Refusing readings of the post as either passé, to which Derrida responds, 'deconstruction began by dying' (1996, p. 225), or as 'triumphant announcement of the death of Marxism' (MacLaren & Farahmandpur, 2000, p. 10), I have echoed Derrida's claim that deconstruction only ever made sense to him as a radicalization of Marx (1994, p. 92).

The ghost of Marx, the work of mourning, the debt to be paid: to return to the quote that begins this essay, perhaps in the interminable task of mourning work in process, the ghost that gives us much to think about and to do is the 'will have been' of the century of Marxism. In the decentering of the *anthropos*, the onto-theological, and the *ego cogito* and its narcissism, Derrida offers a difficult knowledge to those of us who insist on the worldly engagement of deconstruction. Running with concepts that destroy their own names, we seek an unsuccessful and hence possibly faithful mourning to that which we think we cannot think without. This is mourning not as consolation but as a tracing of loss that doubly affirms: both the loss and the still yet of the yes. This is 'affirmation with no ax to grind, affirmation without mastery or mockery, without outcome or end, affirmation without issue ... affirmation without exit' (Krell, 2000, pp. 209, 212).

What all of this means is perhaps best evoked in Pitt and Britzman's (in press) attempt to theorize the qualities of difficult knowledge where they distinguish between 'lovely knowledge' and difficult knowledge. The former reinforces what we think we want from what we find and the latter is knowledge that induces break-downs in representing experience. Here accepting loss becomes the very force of learning and what one loves when lovely knowledge is lost is the promise of thinking and doing otherwise. Such thinking is within and against Enlightenment categories of voice, identity, agency and experience so troubled by incommensurability, historical trauma and the crisis of representation. In the case of Derrida as difficult knowledge, in spite of, perhaps even because of, the critiques of his work too often being based not on a reading of him but on a received version of his ideas, my argument has been that there is plenty of future for Derrida in educational research.[8]

Notes

1. 'Mourning Marxism? Philosophical Explorations in Feminism, Poststructuralism and Education,' Mary Leach, Patti Lather, Kate McCoy, Wanda Pillow and Deborah Britzman, American Educational Research Association (AERA), San Diego, April 1998. The question mark is an homage to a 1972 symposium, Nietzsche Today?, where Derrida presented an early version of his *Spurs* (1979) on questions of Nietzsche and the 'truth' of woman. For an update, see Gallop, 1997, where she asks 'Derrida Today?'

2. '(Mis)Reading Postmodernism: Implications for educational research,' Elizabeth St. Pierre, Bernadette Baker, Wanda Pillow, Patti Lather, and Kate McCoy, AERA, Seattle, April 2001.

3. For a historical survey of the weight of the natural science model on educational research, particularly via a narrowed psychology, see Lagemann, 2000.

4. Rooney is writing about Althusser's reading of Marx as marked by discrepancies, repetitions, hesitations and uncertainties, always beginning again, a doubling between historical situatedness and political interestedness, in short, reading as a necessarily guilty rather than innocent practice.

5. See, for example, Stacey, 1988; Patai, 1991; Opi, 1992; and Fine, 1992.
6. Biddick (1993), in speaking of the disappearing of bodies in imperial social science versus the proliferation of bodies in postcolonial studies, evokes other bodies in tracing the concept to the Mothers of the Disappeared in Chile. Quoting anthropologist Michael Taussig, she notes how the political work of the mothers interrupts public/private distinctions and creates 'a new public ritual whose aim is to allow the tremendous moral and magical power of the unquiet dead to flow into the public sphere, empower individuals, and challenge the would-be guardians of the Nation-State ...' (p. 37).
7. See Lather, 2002, for an exploration of the ethics and politics of this example as a working the ruins of feminist ethnography.
8. Some examples of 'applied Derrida' in educational research include program evaluation (Stronach and MacLure 1997), philosophy of education (Garrison and Leach, 2001), feminist poststructural interventions into a variety of areas (St. Pierre and Pillow, 2000); pedagogy (Trifonas, 2000); and practitioner-oriented research in nursery teaching and math education (Brown and Jones, 2001).

References

Altieri, C. (1990) The Powers and Limits of Oppositional Postmodernism, *American Literary History*, 2, pp. 443–481.

Baker, P. (1995) *Deconstruction and the Ethical Turn* (Gainesville, University Press of Florida).

Balibar, E. (1995) *The Philosophy of Marx*, trans. Chris Turner (London, Verso).

Bennington, G. & Derrida, J. (1991) *Jacques Derrida* (Chicago, University of Chicago Press).

Biddick, K. (1993) Bede's Blush: Postcards from Bali, Bombay, Palo Alto, in: J. Van Engen (ed.), *Past and Future of Medieval Studies* (Notre Dame, IN, University of Notre Dame Press), pp. 16–44.

Bloom, H. (1975) *A Map of Misreading* (New York, Oxford University Press).

Bottomore, T. (1983) *A Dictionary of Marxist Thought* (Oxford, Blackwell Reference).

Brown, T. & Jones, L. (2001) *Action Research and Postmodernism: Congruence and critique* (Buckingham, Open University Press).

Brunette, P. & Wills, D. (1994) *Deconstruction and the Visual Arts: Art, media, architecture* (New York, Cambridge University Press).

Butler, J. (1993) *Bodies that Matter: On the discursive limits of 'sex'* (New York, Routledge).

Caputo, John (ed.) (1997a) *Deconstruction in a Nutshell: A conversation with Jacques Derrida* (New York, Fordham University Press).

Caputo, J. (1997b) Dreaming of the Innumerable: Derrida, Drucilla Cornell, and the dance of gender, in: E. Feder, M. Rawlinson & E. Zakin (eds), *Derrida and Feminism: Recasting the question of woman* (New York, Routledge), pp. 141–160.

Constas, M. (1998) Deciphering Postmodern Educational Research, *Educational Researcher*, 27:9, pp. 37–42.

Derrida, J. (1976) *Of Grammatology* (Baltimore, Johns Hopkins Press).

Derrida, J. (1979) *Spurs: Nietzsche's Styles*, trans. B. Harlow (Chicago, University of Chicago Press).

Derrida, J. (1991) *Cinders* (Lincoln, University of Nebraska Press).

Derrida, J. (1993) The Rhetoric of Drugs: An interview, *differences*, 5:1, pp. 1–25.

Derrida, J. (1994) *Specters of Marx: The state of the debt, the work of mourning, and the new international*, trans. P. Kamuf (New York, Routledge).

Derrida, J. (1996) *As If* I Were Dead: An interview with Jacques Derrida, in: J. Brannigan, R. Robbins & J. Wolfreys (eds), *Applying: To Derrida* (London, Macmillan), pp. 212–226.

Fekete, J. (1992, August) Postmodernism and Cultural Studies (paper presented at the Theory Culture Society conference, Pennsylvania).

Felman, S. & Laub, D. (1992) *Testimony: Crises of Witnessing Literature, Psychoanalysis, and History* (New York, Routledge).

Fine, M. (1992) *Disruptive Voices: The possibilities of feminist research* (Ann Arbor, MI, University of Michigan Press).

Gabardi, W. (2000) *Negotiating Postmodernism* (Minneapolis, University of Minnesota Press).

Gallop, J. (1997) 'Women' in Spurs and Nineties Feminism, in: E. Feder, M. Rawlinson & E. Zakin (eds), *Derrida and Feminism: Recasting the question of woman* (New York, Routledge), pp. 7–20.

Garrison, J. & Leach, M. (2001) Dewey after Derrida, in: V. Richardson, *Handbook of Research on Teaching* (ed.), 4th edn (Washington, DC, AERA), pp. 69–81.

Godzich, W. (1994) *The Culture of Literacy* (Cambridge, MA, Harvard University Press).

Gramsci, A. (1971) *Selections from the Prison Notebooks of Antonio Gramsci*, trans. and ed., Q. Hoare & G. Smith (New York, International Publishers).

Haraway, D. (1997) *Modest Witness@second millenium: Feminism and technoscience* (New York, Routledge).

Haver, W. (1996) *The Body of this Death: Historicity and sociality in the time of AIDS* (Palo Alto, Stanford University Press).

Holland, E. W. (1993) *Baudelaire and Schizoanalysis: The sociopoetics of modernism* (Cambridge, Cambridge University Press).

Howe, K. (1998) The Interpretive Turn and the New Debate in Education, *Educational Researcher*, 27:8, pp. 13–20.

Kearney, R. (1984) *Dialogues with Contemporary Continental Thinkers: The phenomenological heritage* (Manchester, Manchester University Press).

Kincheloe, J. & McLaren, P. (1994) Rethinking Critical Theory and Qualitative Research, in: N. Denzin & Y. Lincoln (eds), *Handbook of Qualitative Research* (Thousand Oaks, CA, Sage).

Krell, D. (2000) *The Purest of Bastards: Works of mourning, art, and affirmation in the thought of Jacques Derrida* (University Park, PA, Pennsylvania State University Press).

Lagemann, E. (2000) *An elusive Science: The troubling history of education research* (Chicago, University of Chicago Press).

Lather, P. (1986) Research as Praxis, *Harvard Educational Review*, 56:3, pp. 257–277.

Lather, P. (1991) *Getting Smart: Feminist research and pedagogy with/in the postmodern* (New York, Routledge).

Lather, P. (2002) Postbook: Working the ruins of feminist ethnography, *Signs: Journal of Women in Culture and Society*, 27:1, pp. 199–227.

Lather, P. & Smithies, C. (1997) *Troubling the Angels: Women living with HIV/AIDS* (Boulder, CO, Westview Press).

Leslie, E. (2000) *Walter Benjamin: Overpowering conformism* (London, Pluto).

Levinson, M. (1995) Pre- and Post-dialectical Materialisms: Modeling praxis without subjects and objects, *Cultural Critique*, Fall, pp. 111–127.

McLaren, P. & Farahmandpur, R. (2000) Reconsidering Marx in post-Marxist Times: A requiem for postmodernism?, *Educational Researcher*, 29:3, 25–33.

Marx, K. (1975) *Early Writings* (London: Penguin).

Opi, Ann (1992) Qualitative Research, Appropriation of the 'Other' and Empowerment, *Feminist Review*, 40, pp. 52–69.

Patai, D. (1991) U.S. Academics and Third World Women: Is ethical research possible?, in: S. Gluck & D. Patai (eds), *Women's Words: The feminist practice of oral history* (New York, Routledge), pp. 137–154.

Pillow, W. (2000) Deciphering Attempts to Decipher Postmodern Educational Research, *Educational Researcher*, 29:5, pp. 21–24.

Pitt, A. & Britzman, D. (in press) Speculations on Qualities of Difficult Knowledge in Teaching and Learning: An experiment in psychoanalytic research, *Qualitative Studies in Education*.

Poster, M. (1989) *Critical Theory and Poststructuralism: In Search of a context* (Ithaca & London, Cornell University Press).

Rooney, E. (1995) Better Read than Dead: Althusser and the fetish of ideology, *Yale French Studies*, 88, pp. 183–200.

Sawiki, J. (1988) In Feminism and the Power of Foucaldian Discourse, in: J. Arac (ed.), *After Foucault: Humanistic knowledge, postmodern challenges* (New Brunswick, NJ, Rutgers University Press), pp. 161–178.

Spanos, W. (1993) *The End of Education: Toward posthumanism* (Minneapolis, University of Minnesota Press).

Spivak, G. (1993) *Outside in the Teaching Machine* (New York, Routledge).

Spivak, G. (1994) Responsibility, *boundary 2*, 21:3, pp. 19–64.

Spivak, G. (1999) *A Critique of Postcolonial Reason: Toward a history of the vanishing present* (Cambridge, MA, Harvard University Press).

Sprinkler, M. (1993) Politics and Friendship: An interview with Jacques Derrida, in: A. Kaplan & M. Sprinkler (eds), *The Althusserean Legacy* (London, Verso), pp. 183–231.

Stacey, J. (1988) Can There Be a Feminist Ethnography?, *Women's Studies International Forum*, 11, pp. 163–182.

St. Pierre, B. (2000) The Call for Intelligibility in Postmodern Educational Research *Educational Researcher*, 29:5, pp. 25–28.

St. Pierre, B. & Pillow, W. (eds) (2000) *Working the Ruins: Feminist poststructural practice and theory in education* (New York, Routledge).

Stronach, I. & MacLure, M. (1997) *Educational Research Undone: The postmodern embrace* (Buckingham, Open University Press).

Tiedemann, Rolf (1989) Historical Materialism or Political Messianism? An interpretation of the theses 'On the concept of history,' in: G. Smith (ed.), *Benjamin: Philosophy, history, aesthetics* (Chicago, University of Chicago Press), 175–202.

Trifonas, P. (2000) *The Ethics of Writing: Derrida, deconstruction and pedagogy* (Lanham, MD, Rowman & Littlefield).

Van Loon, J. (2001) Ethnography: A critical turn in cultural studies, in: Paul Atkinson, Amanda Coffee, Sara Delamont, John Lofland and Lyn Lofland (eds), *Handbook of Ethnography* (London, Sage), pp. 273–284.

Willinsky, J. (2001) The Strategic Education Research Program and the Public Value of Research, *Educational Researcher*, 30:1, pp. 5–14.

3

The Teaching of Philosophy: Renewed rights and responsibilities

DENISE EGÉA-KUEHNE
Louisiana State University

> *Never has philosophy appeared to me as vitally indispensable as today.*
> (Derrida, 2002a)

After twelve years, the long overdue translation of Derrida's *Du droit à la philosophie* has just been made available in English.[1] It is a collection of essays, interviews, and conferences produced by Derrida between 1974 and 1990. They focus on questions of education and research, in schools and universities, with a critical reflection on academic and political institutions, especially on the institutions of philosophy themselves and on the right to access to these institutions and to philosophy. They were selected and gathered by him under a substantial preface titled 'Privilège: Titre justificatif et Remarques introductives.' In this preface, Derrida stressed that

> the common aim of the texts gathered in this collection does not consist in recalling works published elsewhere under the title of deconstruction but in better indicating how deconstruction forces us to *think* differently the institutions of philosophy and the experience of the right to philosophy. (Derrida, 2002b, p. 29/13, his emphasis)

Access to philosophy and right to philosophy and to the teaching of philosophy are more than ever burning topics, requiring renewed thinking in the current context of globalization. Derrida most recently discussed these issues in a May 2002 interview, during a special program on his work aired on French television. In this interview, Derrida precisely talked about the 'privilege' of philosophy, and the necessity of access and of right to philosophy, *today*:

> Never as much as today have I thought that philosophy was indispensable to respond to the most urgent questions of society.... Never have we had such a need for the philosophical memory. (Derrida, 2002a)

Based on a close reading of Derrida's texts, this project proposes to explore the notion of heritage of a 'philosophical memory' before beginning to address the necessity of a right to philosophy and to the teaching of philosophy in the current sociopolitical context, as well as the concurrent call to renewed responsibility.

Heritage

In this same interview in May 2002, Derrida stressed the necessity of a 'philosophical heritage.' Before that, he had admitted recognizing himself—'be it in life or in the work of his thought—in the figure of an heir, and increasingly so' (Derrida & Roudinesco, 2001, p. 15). He has unerringly paid homage to, and 'marked the alliance with,' the philosophers who preceded him: Plato, Descartes, Kant, Nietzsche, Hegel, Heidegger, Husserl, Rousseau, St. Augustine, Jabès, Ceylan, Levinas, Genet, Lacan, Levi-Strauss, Foucault, Althusser, Deleuze, Lyotard, Artaud, Austin and others still. Many a time he has readily acknowledged this heritage as well as the necessity to respond to it. (See, for example, Derrida and Roudinesco, 2001, pp. 11–40.)

Going back to Valéry's *La Liberté de l'esprit* (1939), and to Derrida's discussion of this text in the context of the cultural heritage of Europe, helps understand what Derrida sees behind the notion of heritage. Using a metaphor of economy, Valéry discussed the becoming of culture as a capital in a Europe undergoing major trauma: 'For myself ... it means a capital in the making, which can be used and accumulated, can increase and diminish like any capital you can think of.'[2] In 1939, Valéry saw this capital threatened, in a state of 'crisis,' and warned: 'I declare that our cultural capital is in peril' (Valéry, p. 1090/201/68) He saw this danger coming from the fact that the human factor was missing. He highlighted the need for knowledge and a yearning 'for the power of inner transformation and for a development of sensibilities' (ibid.). Indeed, a heritage is carried by individuals, and in order to keep it alive, they need to know how 'to acquire and exercise the necessary habits, intellectual disciplines, conventions and methods' (ibid.) indispensable to make use of the accumulated capital. The disappearance of those individuals who could keep the memory of a heritage, who knew 'how to read ... how to hear, and even how to listen ... how to see ... to read, hear and see again' is what constitutes the ultimate threat to a cultural heritage (Valéry, cited in Derrida, 1992, p. 70).

Commenting on Valéry's text in *The Other Heading*, Derrida stressed the necessity of a 'responsible memory,' of individuals who are capable of both 'repetition and memory' and who are 'prepared to respond *before*, to respond *of* and to respond *to*, what they had heard, seen, read, and known a first time' (Derrida, 1992, p. 70, his emphasis). It is this repetition, this responsibility toward the cultural capital, which guarantee the growth of a 'universal capital': 'what they insisted on reading again, hearing again or seeing again, was, in return, consolidated into a "solid value." The universal capital grew because of that' (Valéry, p. 1091/202/70).

Derrida suggests that the philosophical heritage is not 'received passively, but as a heritage one calls upon to form new questions or new propositions' (Derrida, 2002a). With a constant reflection fundamental to philosophy, one must put this heritage into question, and re-think the so-called or assumed certainties. This deconstruction, Derrida understands as 'a tension between memory, fidelity, the preservation of something which has been given to us, and at the same time heterogeneity, something absolutely new' (Derrida, 1994a).

A recurring paradox underlies this tension in the necessity to neither accept everything, nor reject everything, to be both faithful and unfaithful to a legacy; i.e.

not to accept a heritage 'passively' as a whole package, but to deconstruct it, to grasp it, understand it through its fractures, its cracks, its gaps, its inconsistencies. It is to know it well enough to be able to unpack its sedimentations, layer by layer—not to destroy the preceding systems of thoughts, but to try to analyze them, to uncover their composition, their presumptions, and their assumptions. For example, when Derrida draws on the philosophers who preceded him, he 'makes [their] works speak within themselves,' extracting their innermost voices 'through their fissures, their blanks, their margins, and their contradictions, without trying to kill them' (Roudinesco, in Derrida & Roudinesco, 2001, p. 13).

Not only does Derrida acknowledge recognizing himself as an heir to the philosophers who preceded him, but he sees it as anything but passive, and he is willing to assume this heritage. For him, this recognition carries the necessity of a response to 'a double injunction, a contradictory assignation' (Derrida & Roudinesco, 2001, p. 15). First we must learn what came 'before us,' and we must reaffirm it: 'we must know, and we must know how to *reaffirm*' (ibid.). Since our heritage comes before us, it comes to us; it is received by us without our being given a chance to choose it. We are born to it, like we are born to our language which is part of it. What is left to us is the power to reaffirm it, that is to accept it, and to confirm it. Yet, not without a critical step. The contradiction Derrida perceives is between 'the passivity of the reception, and the decision to say "yes"' (Derrida & Roudinesco, 2001, p. 16). With this decision, this acceptation, comes the necessity to 'select, filter, interpret, and therefore transform, to not leave intact, undamaged' (ibid.). Secondly, while one reaffirms one's heritage, in order to reaffirm it, at the same time, one must question it, 'reinterpret, critique, displace' it (ibid.). Consequently and paradoxically, one can be faithful to one's heritage only in as much as one accepts to be unfaithful to it, to analyze it, to critique it, to interpret it, relentlessly. Derrida goes one step further, declaring that it is precisely within this heritage that one can find the 'conceptual tools' which will enable one to challenge the very limits of this heritage, as traditionally defined and imposed. Derrida cites the example of human rights which are, by essence, always in the making, 'unfinished,' perfectible beyond their own limits, limits which can be, and should be, constantly pushed (like democracy). Women's rights, children's rights, the right to work, to education, to philosophy, to the teaching of philosophy, and so on, must be 'torn' from the limits of human rights, 'but this movement must be done in the name of an idea/ideal of right already present in the project of the Universal Declaration of the Rights of Man, which was itself founded on the 1789 declaration' (Derrida & Roudinesco, 2001, p. 39).

The choice, if there is a choice, is then given and received through the experience of this reaffirmation and double injunction, experienced anew in each different context through new steps of identification, selection, filtering, and interpretation. In 'The Deconstruction of Actuality,' Derrida explains:

> whoever inherits chooses one spirit rather than another. One makes selections, one filters, one sifts through the ghosts or through the injunctions of each spirit. There is legacy only where assignations are multiple and

contradictory, secret enough to defy interpretation, to carry the unlimited risk of active interpretation. (Derrida, 2002c, p. 111)

To engage oneself as a philosopher, Derrida believes that one 'must do otherwise than merely follow up [*faire du suivisme*] and obey given watchwords or instructions. One must disengage oneself [*se désengager*]' (Derrida, 2002a). The paradox and the danger, the dangerous paradox for a philosopher is that he/she 'can engage politically, *as a philosopher*, only in so far as he/she maintains as much freedom as possible in regards to all that is imposed on him/her as hegemonic discourse, well-received axioms, etc.' (ibid., his emphasis). Derrida perceives his own engagement as concomitant with a necessary autonomy; '[his] political duty as a philosopher' means 'being engaged without alienating [his] freedom, [his] right to disengage' (ibid.). This is closely linked to the aporia of responsible decision (discussed later). However much Derrida can, and is willing to, account for the heterogeneity and complexity of a situation, 'when it is necessary,' he recognizes that there are times 'when an urgent and binary choice' is called for in a specific instance; he believes that it is then his 'duty to respond in a simple [straightforward] fashion,' when it is necessary to take a definite stand, as 'in the case of the Apartheid in South Africa, or for Mumia, or on the death penalty' (ibid.).[3]

Rights

Early on in his career, through both his scholarship and his sociopolitical engagements, Derrida responded to attacks made on philosophy. The texts describing and discussing those were gathered by him in *Du droit à la philosophie*, followed a year later by an address to UNESCO, *Le droit à la philosophie du point de vue cosmopolitique*.[4] Today, threats to philosophy are still at work and renewed in the current sociopolitical context of globalization—what Derrida insists on naming *mondialisation*.[5] Attacks on philosophy are still coming from both governmental institutions (e.g. drive for 'efficiency' and 'accountability') and techno-capitalist society (e.g. selective research funding). Ironically, and as Derrida pointed out when discussing the ' "Haby" project of destruction of philosophy,' such attacks, in fact, stem from and display an unacknowledged philosophical stance (Derrida, 2002c, p. 14). They take place 'in the name of a certain unformulated philosophy,' all the more dangerous since it is ignored on all levels (ibid.).

 Philosophy for everyone is a concept Derrida has held dear for very many years. Besides the numerous texts published, conferences and interviews, there is also, for example, the concrete evidence of the Groupe de Recherches sur l'Enseignement Philosophique (Greph), the États Généraux de la Philosophie (Estates General of Philosophy), and the Collège International de Philosophie (Ciph),[6] 'a college open to philosophical internationality' (Derrida, 2002c, p. 18), where philosophical culture, its heritage and its tradition of questioning, are maintained 'alive and well' (Derrida, 2002c, p. 15) while new modes of thinking and questioning are welcome and encouraged. Derrida has spoken, written, and acted in defense and support of a right of access to philosophy and the teaching of philosophy for all, with no limit on the basis of age, background, language, place, etc. He sees it as 'a matter of keeping the field of tradition open, of making things such that the access to philosophy remains open to the greatest number of people' (ibid.).

Derrida problematized a distinction made by Canguilhem between philosophy's 'own business' and 'the critical philosophy of teaching' which Canguilhem developed in his argument against the Haby Reform (Canguilhem, cited in Derrida, 2002b, p. 44/196). Derrida believed that making such a distinction would be 'paralyzing' and in fact, the Greph endeavored to establish a tight connection between the two and demonstrate its necessity. However, Derrida agreed with Canguilhem's statement that 'the defense of the teaching of philosophy would require a critical philosophy of teaching' (ibid.), recognizing that it expressed one aspect of the Greph's project. Through the Greph, the Estates General, and the Ciph, as well as through his published works and numerous talks and interviews, Derrida's engagement in the teaching of philosophy is well documented, and he has often insisted on 'the necessity of the pedagogical relays that the schools, the university and the media are' (Derrida, 2000, p. 16). For example, in the 1994 Villanova Roundtable Discussion, he talked about his 'struggle ... to impart a space for philosophy teaching and for philosophical research' (Derrida, 1994a), in which philosophy would start being taught earlier in school and would reach across disciplines (again, see the example of the Ciph). In his 2000 interview with *Le Monde de l'Éducation*, he declared: 'The question of teaching runs through all my work and all my politico-institutional engagements, whether they concern schools, the university, or the media' (Derrida, 2000, p. 16). More recently, following up on the deep concern widely expressed in the media as to the ability of politicians to analyze and respond to the major recent sociopolitical developments (widespread corporate corruption and, more tragic still, the US president's push to go to war against Iraq), in the 2002 interview aired on France 3, Charles Pépin asked Derrida whether 'the mighty of this world, heads of states and corporations' should be given access to the teaching of philosophy. Derrida advised not to entertain too many 'illusions as to the organized, institutional, pedagogic form' such a teaching of philosophy could take. But he recognized that 'corporate executives, policy makers, and especially politicians' would benefit from it, in particular since 'all the decisions ... so-called ethical, theo-ethical, which must be taken today, questions of sovereignty, questions of international law, have been the objects of philosophical research for a very long time, and in a renewed fashion now.' In 'Imprévisible liberté,' the same questions were raised concerning the scientists. While making a distinction between 'scientism'[7] and 'science,' Derrida noted that, no matter how competent they may be in their own areas of expertise (while 'competent' and 'areas of expertise' would need further scrutiny) 'sometimes, the "scientists" will proffer any nonsense when they dabble in philosophy or ethics' (Derrida & Roudinesco, 2001, p. 84).

We mentioned earlier that Valéry stressed how in order for philosophical culture not only to 'remain alive and well' (Derrida, 2002c, p. 15) but to grow, it is essential for individuals to learn 'how to read ... how to hear and even how to listen ... how to see ... read, hear and see again' (Valéry, cited in Derrida, 1992, p. 70).

In order for the teaching of philosophy to flourish and grow, one must cultivate the knowledge of one's heritage. One must 'continue to develop, one must continue to read, the relation to tradition must be as cultivated as possible' (Derrida, 2002c, p. 15). But at the same time, while being true to the memory of a culture, to what one receives from the past, while continuing faithfully to preserve and pass along a heritage, the discipline and rigor of the profession, one must also break from the tradition, and strive to inaugurate something new, 'to recast and renew this philosophical treasure' (Derrida, 2002a). The pedagogy involved in the teaching of philosophy cannot be one of mere reproduction, which would soon lead to a closing upon itself and asphyxiation. It must include putting into question past certitudes and assumptions.

The right to philosophy and to the teaching of philosophy carries a right to questioning philosophy. Derrida has widely addressed the mission of the university, and in his May 2002 interview, he recalled what the concept of the university is: 'a place of absolute independence in the questioning and in the quest for truth, in the face of any power, political, economic, religious, etc. That is the concept of the university, the principle of the unconditional freedom of the university.' However, this is an idea, an ideal toward which we must strive, and Derrida recognizes that 'this freedom, in fact, has never been, has never existed' as such. Therefore it has always been important, and now even more than ever, to 'negotiate a relation—which [Derrida] calls, for convenience and brevity's sake, deconstructive—to philosophy in a philosophical place but also a place where philosophy will be put into question' (Derrida, 2002c, p. 18). For example, the Collège International de Philosophie is a place where philosophy is taught, learned, researched, but also challenged, a place where what philosophy is to become and should become in the future, not only in Europe but in the world at large, should also be questioned. The Ciph is one obvious example, but such places can be found and founded elsewhere, within the university and other traditional educational institutions, as well as outside the limits of such institutions. Nearly thirty years after the founding of the Greph, 'The strategy [is still] to keep philosophy open and in lively debate' (Derrida, 2002c, p. 15). In his May 2002 interview, Derrida recalled that the founding principle of the university had a history, a heritage of several centuries, and that if it must be faithful to its principle, it must not only allow questioning, but it must in fact encourage it and nurture it: 'it must not interdict any question, any putting to question, any discourse' within its own borders. That does not mean of course that, within its borders, 'the university [cannot] discuss, fight against, object, contest,' these questions and discourses. But they should not be excluded from inside the university, especially not according to 'criteria external to the university,' whether these criteria are issued from governmental, techno-scientific, or economic concerns (Derrida, 2002a).

Responsibilities

This questioning of philosophy, from within and from outside its margins, is perceived by Derrida as a most compelling responsibility: '[a] philosopher is always someone for whom philosophy is not a *given*, someone who, in essence, must question the essence and the purpose of philosophy. And re-invent it' (Derrida, 2002c, p. 332). The philosopher has a duty which entails the risk of asking questions which are unsettling (*dérangeantes*), which challenge established traditions, beliefs and certitudes. 'There is danger in thinking' said Derrida in his May 2002 interview, and 'it is first the danger to which I expose myself.' He explained that the goal is not to frighten, but rather 'to have it out with what in the thinkable remains unthinkable, or in any case threatening, unsettling, and there, for [him], is the criteria of the experience of thinking.' Assuming the responsibility of this risk is the responsibility of the philosopher, a responsibility anyone claiming a right to philosophy or to the teaching of philosophy must assume, a responsibility which is the essence of philosophy and the teaching of philosophy. In the *Le Monde de l'Éducation* interview, Derrida addressed the philosopher's pedagogical responsibilities. For him, 'the task is infinite,' with a necessity sometimes to simplify in order to be able to transmit knowledge, but also a necessity 'to refine ever more scrupulously' his thought. To this necessity, which he understands as a responsibility, he opposes that of 'not waiting, and at a precise moment, here, now, to take the risk (weighing it as best as possible) to speak, to teach, to publish' (Derrida, 2000, p. 18). In the traditional model of the intellectual, Derrida sees 'a guardian held responsible for the memory and culture,' but also 'a citizen entrusted with a sort of spiritual mission' (Derrida, 1992, p. 23). No doubt, with its memory we are also given the responsibility of this legacy, a responsibility—Derrida pointed out—which we did not choose.

Derrida described this responsibility toward a legacy as dual, as a duty to both keep and renew. This is not without risk either. Discussing European culture, Derrida stressed that an important characteristic of culture is that its history indicates a direction, 'no doubt presupposes an identifiable heading, a *telos* toward which the movement, the memory and the promise, the identity—even if it were as difference to/with oneself—dreams of gathering itself' (Derrida, 1992, pp. 17–18). For Derrida it is 'necessary to anticipate, to keep the heading [*garder le cap*],' to maintain the direction, the goals, lest we repeat what has occurred before: under the guise of 'the absolutely new, we may fear to see reappear the ghost of the worst [evils], the one which has already been identified' as such (ibid., p. 18). Examples abound, especially in education, of the 'new' which is nothing but a repetition of the old rhetoric. On the other hand, history presupposes that we have no knowledge of the future, no way to anticipate, identify before the fact: 'the unicity of the other *today* should be awaited *as such* ... it should be anticipated *as* the unforeseeable, the *unanticipatable*, the non-masterable, non-identifiable, in short, as that of which one has yet no memory' (ibid., Derrida's emphasis). This is precisely what constitutes the event.

Consequently, Derrida warns, our responsibility entails being wary of '*both* repetitive memory, *and* ... the absolutely new' (Derrida, 1992, p. 19, his emphasis). We must be vigilant about '*both* anamnestic capitalization *and* the amnesic exposure to what would no longer be identifiable at all' (ibid., his emphasis). The difficulty is in assuming a responsibility which is double and contradictory, for, while we must preserve and guard an ideal of culture, we must also remain aware that a culture (be it of Europe or any other culture) 'consists precisely in not closing itself upon its own identity, and in proceeding in an exemplary fashion toward what it is not ... indeed ... perhaps something else altogether' (Derrida, 1992, p. 29).

Double injunctions, contradictions, aporias are, for Derrida, the essence of responsibility. He has described and discussed extensively and in most of his texts how these dilemmas are inherent in the concept of responsibility, are in fact *the very condition* of its possibility. For 'at a certain point, the promise and the decision, that is to say the responsibility, owe their possibility to the test of undecidability which will always remain their condition' (Derrida, 1994b, p. 126). He stressed repeatedly that, if there is an easy decision to make, there is, in fact, no decision to be made; if the decision is thought to be known, there is no decision, therefore, no responsibility to be taken, only a set of rules to follow, or a program to implement. Decisions are made outside the realm of knowledge. Derrida described how, 'from the knowledge to the decision, a leap is required, even if one must know as much and as well as possible before making a decision' (Derrida & Roudinesco, 2001, p. 92). For example, in both cases, it is assumed that scientists and politicians have the philosophical, ethical, political or juridical 'competence' besides the necessary knowledge in their respective fields. But even if their competence, knowledge and lucidity are established, those are neither sufficient nor adequate since responsible decisions are not of the order of knowledge or competence; they are 'not programmable by any knowledge, not by science or consciousness' (Derrida, 2002c, p. 372; see also Derrida & Roudinesco, 2001, p. 92). In 1991, in an interview with François Ewald which took place shortly after the launching of the Gulf war,[8] Derrida commented on a situation eerily similar to the current one, where politicians are struggling to make a momentous decision:

> No matter how necessary and rigorous the case one makes against Western, Israeli, and Arab-Islamic politics (besides, there is more than one [politics] in each category), no matter how far back one wants to and *must* go in these proceedings (and one must go back very, very far, in articulated stages), the decision to be made (embargo or no embargo, war or no war, this or that 'war goal') has to be made within a 'today,' at one unique moment when no past error can be erased any longer, nor even repaired. This terrifying strategic wager can be guaranteed in advance by nothing, not even by the reckoning (always necessarily speculative) that a contrary wager would have led to the worst. (Derrida, 2001c, p. 71)

Any responsibility implies a dilemma, a dual obligation, whose aspects are both contradictory and conflictual. In all cases, it is necessary to go through antinomies in order to take into consideration the uniqueness of each situation and its complexity. Each time, it is necessary to reinvent what responsibilities are involved, to 'invent for [oneself] a rule of transaction, of compromise, of negotiation which is not programmable,' in order to respond to the singularity of the event—not by ignoring previously developed concepts (e.g. duty to knowledge), but by going beyond them. This dual obligation, contradictory and conflictual, is inherent in

Derrida's concept of responsibility, as opposed to a moral or political technique. In facing such responsibility, there is no guarantee, no certitude of a unique pat successful solution. Derrida proposed to call it 'a profession of faith,' when

> an infinite leap still remains before me, because a responsible decision, if it is to be the event of a decision in the face of two contradictory imperatives, cannot simply be dictated, programmed, prescribed by knowledge as such. This is why I am tempted to speak of a *profession of faith*. (Derrida, 2002c, p. 372, his emphasis)

Derrida links this concept—this condition of possibility as being dependent on the simultaneous necessity of a condition of impossibility—to a notion of 'messianism,' to the experience of the promise. It is by opening a space for the affirmation of this promise, of the 'messianic and emancipatory promise,' of the impossible event as a promise, that it will preserve its capital of possibilities, of dynamic ideal in-the-making, to-come. There is danger in settling for an easy consensus, for 'transparency,' since while 'claiming to speak in the name of intelligibility, good sense, common sense, or [supposedly] the democratic ethic, this discourse tends, by means of these very things, and as if naturally, to discredit anything which complicates this model' (Derrida, 1992, p. 55; see also Egéa-Kuehne, 1995, 1997). As soon as we settle for a common space, we turn all possibilities into a program or into an 'onto-theological or teleo-eschatological scheme' (Derrida, 1994b, p. 126). Derrida defines responsibility as 'a certain experience and experiment of the possibility of the impossible: the testing of the aporia from which one may invent the only possible invention, the impossible invention' (Derrida, 1992, p. 41). He also shows how closely related aporia, responsibility, and ethics are, declaring: 'ethics, politics and responsibility, *if there are any*, will only ever have begun with the experience and the experiment of the aporia' (ibid.).

New Responsibilities for the Philosopher and the Teaching of Philosophy

In a 1999 talk before UNESCO[9] which addressed the general theme of 'The New World Contract' being drawn up by Federico Mayor, then Director General of the Institution, Derrida discussed 'the task of the philosopher here, such as [he saw] it assigned and implied by the new "world contract"' (Derrida, 2002c, p. 376). Derrida understood this task as also being 'that of whoever tends to assume political and legal responsibilities in this matter' (ibid.). He gave as examples four of the tightly linked themes around which have revolved his lectures, seminars, conferences, publications and interviews (including several interventions before UNESCO) in the most recent years: work, forgiveness, peace, and the death penalty.[10]

Indeed, in his 2002 interview with France 3, Derrida insisted that philosophy is more necessary than ever to respond to the most urgent questions raised by today's sociopolitical context, questions of politics, ethics and especially rights and law. These issues concern international institutions, including 'the UN, the

Security Council, the role of certain sovereign states in their relation of respect or non-respect toward these international institutions' (i.e. Apartheid, crimes against humanity, the death penalty, children's exploitation, etc.) all having to do with international law (see also Derrida, 2001). Derrida stressed that, if international law is to be modified, 'it can be done only on the grounds of a philosophical reflection' (Derrida, 2002a). Other vital issues concerning cloning, genetic research, organ transplant, animals, and so on, also require a questioning and a reflection guided by the philosophical model, and the philosophical heritage is indispensable to inform a responsible response.

Another point Derrida makes, referring to Kant's 1784 text *Idee zu einer allgemeinen Geschichte in weltbürgerlicher Absicht*,[11] is that these institutions as well as international law, most of which appeared after the Second World War,

> are already *philosophemes*. They are philosophical acts and archives, philosophical productions and products not only because the concepts that legitimate them have an ascribable *philosophical history* and thus a philosophical history that finds itself inscribed in the charter of UNESCO; rather because, at the same time, and for this reason, such institutions imply the sharing of a culture and a philosophical language, committing themselves consequently to making possible, and first through education [*et d'abord par l'éducation*], the access to this language and to this culture. (Derrida, 2002c, p. 331, his emphasis)[12]

When signing the charter of such an institution,[13] a state and its people make a commitment to uphold the culture, the philosophical heritage thus inscribed in its charter. Derrida pointed out that some may see in it an 'infinite opening,' while others might object that it is limiting to an apparently essentially European heritage (Derrida, 2002c, p. 331).[14] And then some may lose sight of this implicit commitment altogether. Which stresses all the more that this commitment entails an education to culture and to philosophy which is of paramount importance for an understanding of what is at stake, and which is 'indispensable to the understanding and the implementation of these commitments to these international institutions, which are ... philosophical in essence' (ibid.).

In the current sociopolitical context, in the light of the acute pressure of current conflicts in the Middle East and Eastern Europe and the rhetoric of war, more than ever, Derrida's questions (though over 10 years old, but asked in the context of a similar conflict) sound most urgent:

> What are the concrete stakes of this situation today? Why must the important questions concerning philosophical teaching and research, why must the imperative of the right to philosophy be deployed in their international dimension today more than ever? Why are the responsibilities which need to be taken no longer—and even less today in the twenty-first century—simply national? What do 'national,' 'cosmopolitan,' 'universal' mean here for, and with regard to, philosophy, philosophical research, philosophical education or training, or even for a philosophical question

or practice that would not be essentially linked to research or education? (Derrida, 2002c, p. 332)

In this context, Derrida had already pointed out, the right to philosophy and to the teaching of philosophy, as well as the responsibilities at stake must be considered beyond national borders, on a cosmopolitan and universal level. This position raises new questions, already discussed by Kant who stated that 'a philosophical approach to universal history ... is inseparable from a kind of plan of nature that aims for a total, perfect political unification of the human species (*die vollkommene bürgerliche Vereinigung in der Menschengattung*)' (Derrida, 2002c, p. 333). Since then, such institutions as UNESCO, the UN, and the Security Council have moved the creation of 'institutions ruled by international—and thus philosophical—law' out of the realm of 'fiction' into that of actual facts (ibid.). Whether they, that is their members who signed their charters, uphold the commitment thus made is at issue.[15]

One of the responsibilities of today's philosopher, in the context of globalization, is the necessity to move beyond the opposition Eurocentrism vs. anti-Eurocentrism. While upholding the memory of a philosophical heritage essentially Euro-Christian (Greek, Roman, Jewish, Christian and Islamic, or Mediterranean/Central European, or Greco-Roman-Arab/Germanic), it is necessary to both recognize its origins, and go beyond its limits. It is also essential to be aware that the philosophical has been and is being transformed and appropriated by non-European languages and cultures. According to Derrida, this is what a close, 'long and slow' study of the historical roots and development of philosophy, one which is in progress, will reveal. He believes that

> What is happening today, and has been for some time ... are philosophical formations that will not let themselves be contained in this dialectic, which is basically cultural, colonial and neo-colonial, of appropriation and alienation. There are other ways [*voies*] of philosophy. ... [Moreover, n]ot only are there other ways of philosophy, but philosophy, if there is such a thing, is the other way [*l'autre voie*]. (Derrida, 2002c, p. 337)

Derrida also believes that letting philosophy, even under the label of cosmopolitanism, be determined by the opposition Eurocentrism vs. non-Eurocentrism would be limiting the right to philosophy and to the teaching of philosophy. In order to follow up and understand 'what is happening and can still happen under the name of philosophy,' Derrida suggests three fields of reflection, under three 'titles.' According to him, they 'could be the concrete conditions for respect and for the extension of the right to philosophy.'

1. *First title.* Whoever thinks that the right to philosophy from a cosmopolitan point of view must be respected, granted, extended will have to take into account the competition that exists and has always existed between several models, styles, philosophical traditions.

2. *Second title.* The respect and extension of the right to philosophy to all people also presupposes ... the appropriation but also the overflowing of what are said to be ... the founding or originary languages of philosophy—the Greek, Latin, Germanic or Arabic languages.

3. *Third title.* Although philosophy does not simply amount to its institutional or pedagogical moments, nonetheless the many differences of tradition, style, language, and philosophical nationality are translated or embodied in the institutional or pedagogical models, at times even produced by those structures.

(Derrida, 2002c, pp. 337–340)

Conclusion

In the current context of globalization and sociopolitical conflicts, rights to philosophy and the teaching of philosophy take a new dimension and urgency, and present new challenges. Reading Derrida helps understand the importance and the necessity of our philosophical heritage. At the same time, it makes clear that one of the responsibilities of today's philosopher, while affirming the essentially Western philosophical heritage, is to move beyond 'the old, tiresome, wearing, wearying opposition between Eurocentrism and anti-Eurocentrism' (Derrida, 2002c, p. 336). Declaring philosophy to be cosmopolitan is not sufficient to make it universal. One must recognize the role played by appropriation and transformation of the philosophical and of the institutional and pedagogical models in non-European languages and cultures. Today, access and rights to philosophy and the teaching of philosophy are ever more necessary, for they are indispensable to understand our renewed responsibilities and to make responsible decisions.

Notes

1. Derrida, 2002b. This is the first part of a two-volume translation of *Du droit à la philosophie* (Paris, Galilée, 1990). The second half will be published in a subsequent volume titled *Eyes of the University: Right to Philosophy II.* In references to this work, the first number refers to the French text, the second to the English translation (up to p. 280 of the French edition).

2. Valéry, 1960, p. 1089; Valéry, 1962, p. 200; cited in Derrida, 1992, p. 66. The translation is slightly modified; the first number will refer to the French text, the second to the Folliot & Mathews's English translation, the third to the citation in *The Other Heading,* when applicable.

3. Examples of Derrida's political engagement are numerous throughout the years, be it Apartheid in South Africa, Mumia Abu-Jamal, the death penalty, or as recalled by Giesbert in this interview, his imprisonment in Prague.

4. Introductory address to a conference sponsored by UNESCO on 23 May 1991, published by Presses Universitaires de France in 1997. English translation by E. Rottenberg (2002), 'The Right to Philosophy from a Cosmopolitan Point of View,' in Derrida, 2002c, pp. 329–342.

5. Derrida has explained his preference for this term on several occasions, even his use of *mondialatinisation* (Derrida, 2001a, p. 48). See, for example, Derrida, 2002c, pp. 374–375, and Derrida, 2002d, p. 203.

6. For a detailed description of the activities of the Greph, Ciph and Estates General of Philosophy, see Derrida, 2002b, especially pp. 24–41/10–22, and 239–278/164–192. See also Derrida, 2002c, pp. 14–22.

7. Term generalized after 1911, referring to the belief that Science (i.e. all sciences) could explain, resolve and control all human phenomena. It became 'a discourse on science which claims to abolish philosophy while deploying the very discourse of science,' in Lecourt, 1999, p. 852.

8. 'On the eve of this phase of the war strangely named the "ground" war [*guerre terrestre*].'

9. 'La mondialisation et la paix cosmopolitique' was first delivered at UNESCO's headquarters in Paris on 6 November 1999, as part of the 'Discussions of the Twenty-first Century;' transcribed and published in *Regards*, 54 (February 2000), pp. 16–19; translated by Elizabeth Rottenberg, in Derrida, 2002d, pp. 371–386.

10. UNESCO has deemed it necessary to establish for itself a department of philosophy, which is why, in a previous address before UNESCO, in 1991, Derrida declared that 'UNESCO may in fact be this privileged place ... perhaps the only possible place in which to truly deploy the question' of the right to philosophy. He continued: 'As if, in a word, UNESCO and, within UNESCO in a way that was privileged, its department of philosophy, were, if I can say this, the singular *emanation* of something like *philosophy* as "a right to philosophy from a cosmopolitan point of view"' (Derrida, 2002c, p. 330, his emphasis).

11. *Idea* [in view of] of *a Universal History with a Cosmopolitan Purpose*.

12. Translation slightly modified to reflect the fact that, in the French text, 'first of all' relates to 'education' (thus emphasizing the importance of education) and not to 'access' to language and culture.

13. Following an eighteen-years absence from UNESCO, on 12 September 2002, speaking before the UN General Assembly, President Bush announced the return of the United States of America to UNESCO (188 Member States; as a founding member, the United States helped shape the 1945 Constitution). See UNESCO, 2002.

14. See also pp. 371–386. They may overlook the fact that this is no simple heritage, and 'combines and accumulates powerful traditions within it' (Derrida, 2001b, p. 31). See also, for example, Derrida & Roudinesco, 2001 and Derrida, 2001a.

15. In fact, as I put the final period to this paragraph, NPR started interviews with three 'experts' on President Bush's pressure to go into war against Iraq regardless of the UN and other Member States' respective positions, not to mention the United States Congress's own position.

References

Derrida, J. (1992) *The Other Heading: Reflections on Today's Europe*, trans. P. A. Brault & M. B. Nass (Bloomington & Indianapolis, Indiana University Press).

Derrida, J. (1994a) Roundtable Discussion with Jacques Derrida, Villanova University, 3 October 1994, <http://www.hydra.umn.edu/derrida/vill.html>.

Derrida, J. (1994b) *Specters of Marx*, trans. P. Kamuf (New York & London, Routledge).

Derrida, J. (2000) Autrui est secret parce qu'il est autre, *Le Monde de l'Éducation*, 284, pp. 14–21. Reprinted in '21 penseurs pour comprendre le XXIe siècle ... et 21 regards critiques', Numéro Spécial, *Le Monde de l'Education*, 194 (2001), pp. 104–112. Trans Egéa-Kuehne.

Derrida, J. (2001a) *Foi et Savoir, suivi de Le Siècle et le Pardon* (Paris, Seuil).

Derrida, J. (2001b) *On Cosmopolitanism and Forgiveness* (London & New York, Routledge).

Derrida, J. (2001c) 'A Certain "Madness" Must Watch Over Thinking', trans. D. Egéa-Kuehne, in: Biesta, G. J. J. and Egéa-Kuehne, D. (eds), *Derrida & Education* (London & New York, Routledge). First published in a special issue of the *Magazine Littéraire*, 286 (1991), pp. 18–30.

Derrida, J. (2002a) Culture et dépendences—Spécial Jacques Derrida, presented by F.-O. Giesbert, with the participation of E. Levy, C. Pépin, D. Schick & S. Werba (France 3 Television, May 2002). Not available in print. Trans. D. Egéa-Kuehne.

Derrida, J. (2002b) *Who's Afraid of Philosophy?: Right to Philosophy 1*, trans. J. Plug (Stanford, Stanford University Press).

Derrida, J. (2002c) *Negotiations: Interventions and Interviews, 1971–2001*, trans. and intro. E. Rottenberg (Stanford, Stanford University Press).

Derrida (2002d) *Without Alibi*, trans. P. Kamuf (Stanford, Stanford University Press).

Derrida, J. & Roudinesco, E. (2001) *De quoi demain … Dialogue* (Paris, Fayard/Galilée).

Egéa-Kuehne, D. (1995) Deconstruction Revisited and Derrida's Call for Responsibility, *Educational Theory*, 45:3, pp. 293–309.

Egéa-Kuehne, D. (1997) Neutrality in Education and Derrida's Call for 'Double Duty,' in: F. Margonis (ed.), *Philosophy of Education 1996* (Urbana, IL, Philosophy of Education Society), pp. 154–163.

Lecourt, D. (ed.) (1999) *Dictionnaire d'histoire et de philosophie des sciences* (Paris, Presses Universitaires Françaises).

UNESCO (2002) Press Release no. 2002–64, Paris, 12 September 2002, <http://www.unesco.org>.

Valéry, P. (1960) Notes sur la grandeur et la décadence de l'Europe, in: *Oeuvres Complètes*, vol. 2 (Paris, Pléiade).

Valéry, P. (1962) *History and Politics*, trans. D. Folliot & J. Mathews (New York, Bollingen).

4

The Ethics of Science and/as Research: Deconstruction and the orientations of a new academic responsibility

PETER TRIFONAS

Institute for Studies in Education / University of Toronto

Knowledge and Interests: The reason and responsibility of research within the university

The principle of reason 'as principle of grounding, foundation or institution' (Derrida, 1983) has tended to guide the science of research toward techno-practical ends (see Derrida, 1983). From this epistemic superintendence of the terms of knowledge and inquiry, there has arisen the traditional notion of academic responsibility that is tied to the pursuit of truth via a conception of science based on the teleological orientation of intellectual labour toward the production of tangible outcomes achieved according to a method of procedural objectivity (Trifonas, 1996, 1998, 1999, 2000a, 2000b, 2001).

For Jacques Derrida, this is not an insignificant historicity because its effects determine the nature of the epistemic subjectivity of the researcher. The ethics and politics of research—and the role 'the ["modern"] university may play' (Derrida, 1983, p. 11) in helping to construct the dimensions of a scholastic arena impelled toward the quest for the pragmatic application of results or the 'pay off' (ibid., p. 12) of pre-directed outcomes of inquiry—is fed more and more by competing interests situated outside of the rationale of the institution itself. Most certainly, academic work 'programmed, focused, organized' (ibid., p. 11) solely on the future expectation of its profitable utilisation, does not and cannot take into account the democratic ideals protecting the welfare of the nation-state, especially when the quest for knowledge becomes driven by particularised and exclusionary agendas arbitrarily guiding the course of inquiry for political or economic reasons. A myopic orientation to research as an instrumental process of usable outcomes limits intellectual freedom and responsibility because it is, Derrida has contended, 'centered instead on [the desires of] multinational military-industrial complexes of techno-economic networks, or rather international technomilitary networks that are apparently multi- or trans-national in form'.[1] Indeed, such regulatory forces wielding the power of 'in-vest-ment'—not necessarily monetary—are always wanting to control the mechanisms of creative production to commodify knowledge so as to make it a useful product of pre-ordained and pre-conceived epistemological directives and scientific outcomes not necessarily for the sake of science, truth or knowledge. These 'external' influences affecting and reflecting the purposes of the university are to be found more and more in not so obvious, but covertly strategic, areas within the architectonical confines of the traditional institutional structure. This is possible thanks to the 'channel of private foundations' (ibid., p. 14) that have penetrated the sphere of the modern research university and are therefore indispensable to the logic of its goals and operation. In fact, the direction and scope of research within and throughout the university institution are guided by the irresistible lure of funding and other personal and professional incentives arising therefrom (e.g. power, status, career advancement).

And yet, to intimate, as I have, that the 'pragmatic' (utilitarian) interests of an 'applied science' are in opposition to the relative disinterestedness of 'fundamental' (basic) inquiry is to create a binary distinction. A qualitative and evaluative division of research along these lines is, without a doubt, problematic. The ethics of its logic is something that deconstruction has shown can and should consistently be worked against. Derrida reminds us, however, that such a metaphysical conceit separating theory and practice is of 'real but limited relevance' (ibid., p. 12): given that the deferred dividends of the 'detours, delays and relays of "orientation," its more random aspects' (ibid., p. 12), are either incalculable or go unrecognised until a suitable situation of the advantageous use of research presents itself. The use-value of research cannot be an unimportant consideration because the ethics of science and its endeavours quickly occupies the foreground of analysis as the purpose of knowledge discovery comes into question. For Derrida, it is naïve to believe there are some 'basic disciplines ["philosophy," "theoretical physics," and "pure mathematics" are the examples he gives] shielded from power, inaccessible to programming by the pressures of the State or, under cover of the State, by civil society or capital interests' (ibid., p. 12). That thought has now been unthinkable for some time, especially since the monstrous dawning of the 'post-critical' age of nuclear politics and the wake of the informatising function of science as research 'At the service of war' (ibid., p. 13). In this sense, what has been at stake with respect to the purpose of research in all of its manifestations as a mode of conquering the symbiotic field of the human and non-human Other, concerns the 'control' of knowledge and the industry or commodification of its results as intellectual by-products to be used by the State apparatus. This desire to command the path and ethics of science has and will pivot around the 'higher priority' issue of protecting 'national and international security' (ibid., p. 13) interests, however heterogeneous the calculation of a plan of insurance or the lack of it is to the logic of 'peace' or 'democracy'.

The differentiation of the aims of research is not that discreet an indicator of its 'use-value' so as to clearly distinguish between the profitability of application and the destructive effects of misappropriation, despite the usual factoring-in of 'reasonable' margins of error. Derrida comments,

> research programs have to [in the sense of, *are made to*] encompass the entire field of information, the stockpiling of knowledge, the workings and thus also the essence of language and of all semiotic systems, translation, coding and decoding, the play of presence and absence, hermeneutics, semantics, structural and generative linguistics, pragmatics, rhetoric. I am

accumulating all these disciplines in a haphazard way, on purpose, but I shall end with literature, poetry, the arts, fiction in general: the theory that has all these discipline as its object may be just as useful in ideological warfare as it is in experimentation with variables in all-too-familiar perversions of the referential function. Such a theory may always be put to work in communications strategy, the theory of commands, the most refined military pragmatics of jussive utterances (by what token, for example, will it be clear that an utterance is to be taken as a command in the new technology of telecommunications? How are the new resources of simulation and simulacrum to be controlled? And so on ...) ... Furthermore, when certain random consequences of research are taken into account, it is always possible to have in view some eventual benefit that may ensue from an apparently useless research project (in philosophy or the humanities, for example). The history of the sciences encourages researchers to integrate that margin of randomness into their centralized calculation. They then proceed to adjust the means at their disposal, the available financial support, and the distribution of credits. A State power or forces that it represents no longer need to prohibit research or to censor discourse, especially in the West. It is enough that they can limit the means, can regulate support for production, transmission, diffusion. (ibid., p. 13)

Within the 'concept of information or informatization' (ibid., p. 13), the ethics and the politics of research take shape essentially as the conservative ideal of 'Science' the university itself stands on is overtaken. The transformation of research goals and purposes consumes the institution because the autonomy of its own self-regulating measures of knowledge advancement is sacrificed to the real-world pressures of simply securing a sustainable future for itself as an economically and politically viable institution of culture. And that is understandable, although it may not be ethically defensible or acceptable. Not even to those unquestioning defenders of the dominant (or onto-teleological) interpretation of the principle of reason and science the university is grounded on: essentially by its logic of 'integrat[ing] the basic to the oriented, the purely rational to the technical, thus bearing witness to that original intermingling of the metaphysical and the technical' (ibid., p. 14) within the disciplinary corpus of the institution.

Deconstruction and Rethinking the Ground of Academic Responsibility

The academic responsibility Derrida has wished to 'awaken or resituate' (ibid., p. 14) is 'in the university or before (*devant*) the university, whether one belongs to it or not' (ibid., p. 14). *Its double gesture bridges the ungrounded space of the conditions of possibility over which positions on ethics and responsibility, reason and rationality are thought out and taken.* The difficulty of this 'new academic responsibility' is elaborated, according to Derrida, by actively opposing the 'prohibiting limitations' (ibid., p. 13) that 'presses, [public and private] foundations, mass media' (ibid.,

p. 13) and other 'interest groups' place on the act of research within the institution: 'The unacceptability of a discourse, the non-certification of a research project, the illegitimacy of a course offering are declared by evaluative actions: studying such evaluations is, it seems to me [he emphasizes], one of the tasks most indispensable to the exercise of academic responsibility, most urgent for the maintenance of its dignity' (ibid., p. 13). To intervene decisively in the business of the university is to appeal (to) reason, to ask for the concession of reasons out of which to judge judgements made in the name of truth and the imperative for gaining knowledge.

The medium in question that relates the obligation and responsibility of ethics to politics and the practices of the institution is language and two ways of thinking about the *value of language*. Derrida defines these complementary modes of thought in relation to the principle of reason as 'instrumental' (informative) and 'poietic' (creative), essentially by associating their contrasting methods of semiological effect (e.g. representation/undecidability) with research-type, end-oriented and funda-mental. On the basis of the difference of values of finitude that must not proceed from knowledge but always head toward the possibility of its re-invention, is grounded the deconstructive attempt to define a new academic responsibility 'in the face of the university's total subjection to the technologies of informatization' (ibid., p. 14). The cross-contamination between the 'instrumental' and the '*poietic*' aims of research science is obvious 'at the outer limits of the authority and power of the principle of reason' (ibid., p. 14) where the specificity of goals or purposes is blurred by the shared logic of *praxis*. Derrida situates this antinomic responsibility— of 'the experience and experiment of the *aporia*' (Derrida, 1992, p. 41), more or less—within the general domain a hypothetical 'community of thought' that is committed to the 'sounding [of] a call to practice it' (Derrida, 1983, p. 16). The '*group-at-large*' referred to is not one 'of research, of science, of philosophy, since these values [of "professionalism" and "disciplinarity" no matter how "radical"] are most often subjected to the unquestioned authority of the principle of reason' (ibid., p. 16) and can be absorbed into the homogeneous magma of intra-institutional discourse (e.g. the standardisation of Marxism and psychoanalysis). Derrida has named this loosely gathered consortium a 'community of the question' (Derrida, 1978) after the death of philosophy, a chance for safekeeping the possibility of the question of the *violence of metaphysics*, onto-theo-logical and proto-ethical. How would it function? Derrida explains as follows:

> Such a community would interrogate the essence of reason and of the principle of reason, the values of the basic, of the principial, of radicality, of the *arkhe* in general, and it would attempt to draw out all the possible consequences of this questioning. It is not certain that such a thinking can bring together a community or found an institution in the traditional sense of these words. What is meant by community and institution must be rethought. This thinking must also unmask—an infinite task—all the ruses of end-orienting reason, the paths by which apparently disinterested research can find itself indirectly reappropriated, reinvested by programs of all sorts. That does not mean that 'orientation' is bad in itself and that

it must be combatted, far from it. Rather, I am defining the necessity for a new way of educating students that will prepare them to undertake new analyses in order to evaluate these ends and choose, when possible, among them all. (Derrida, 1983, p. 16)

The Affirmative Ethics and Academic Responsibility of Deconstruction in Practice: The International College of Philosophy

Less than a year after the above comment, the *Collège Internationale de Philosophie* (CIPH) would open its doors to students and scholars (during January of 1984), providing perhaps a much-anticipated answer to the biding dilemma of a 'community of the question' and the suggestion of a rethinking of the institution of 'higher' education.[2] Derrida was its first 'Acting Director', to be followed by Jean-François Lyotard and others in a succession of one-year appointments. The international make-up of the CIPH was and is reflected by the composition of the membership of its 'governing bodies', the result of an open letter reprinted on the French Ministry of Research and Industry letterhead and circulated around the world in May 1982, to invite the participation of interested parties in its planning and operation.[3] There were more than 750 replies to the epistle Derrida drafted on behalf of the Socialist government of François Mitterrand, who, on the eve of his election to office, had promised the GREPH that he would protect the discipline of Philosophy within the organisation of the public school and university curricula. All responses were evaluated and the four members of the mission (Derrida, François Châtelet, Jean-Pierre Faye and Dominique Lecourt) issued the lengthy *Rapport pour le Collège International de Philosophie* (Derrida *et al.*, 1982). The express intention or 'regulating idea' of that document was to interrogate and displace 'the ontological encyclopaedic model by which the philosophical concept of the *universitas* has been guided for the last two centuries' (Derrida, 1990, p. 13) as was originally stated in the letter:

> The International College of Philosophy is to give (*doit donner*) priority to themes, problems, experiences that do not yet find a legitimate or sufficient place in other institutions, whether they concern philosophy or the relations between philosophy, sciences, techniques, and artistic productions. Beyond simple interdisciplinarity, it will be oriented toward new intersections and will work to open (*frayer*) other paths between constituted or compartmentalized disciplines (*savoirs*). In order to undo traditional isolations, the college will be broadly open, according to new modes, to exchanges from abroad. (cited in Leitch, 1986, pp. 103–104)

That the institution was to be a 'College of Philosophy' is not incidental, secondary or superfluous to a consideration of the ethics and politics of research and the being of the university. The semiologico-symbolic inter-ground of any and all potential articulations of academic responsibility is, for Derrida, an irreducible dimension of 'thought' and 'thinking' analogous with the poststructural meta-criticality of deconstruction. It is an intellectual practice of grafting, confrontation, and productive interference that transgresses the fixed borders of 'the arts' and 'the sciences' for the transformative redistribution of knowledge values and the founding of new fields of research at the inter-spaces of philosophy and science. This is made explicit by Derrida's (quasi-)deconstruction of the interdisciplinary schematicism of the Kantian university model:

> One can no longer distinguish between technology on the one hand and theory, science and rationality on the other. ... [A]n essential affinity ties together objective knowledge, the principle of reason, and a certain metaphysical determination of the relation to truth. ... One can no longer maintain the boundary that Kant, for example, sought to establish between the schema that he called 'technical' and the one he called 'architectonic' in the systematic organization of knowledge—which was also to ground a systematic organization of the university. The architectonic is the art of systems. 'Under the government of reason, our knowledge in general,' Kant says, 'should not form a rhapsody, but it must form a system in which alone it can support and favour the essential aims of reason.' To that pure rationality of the architectonic, Kant opposes the scheme of the merely technical unity that is empirically oriented, according to views and ends that are incidental, not essential. It is thus a limit between two aims that Kant seeks to define, the essential and noble end of reason that gave rise to fundamental science versus the incidental and empirical ends that can be systematized only in terms of technical schemas and necessities. (Derrida, 1983, p. 12)

Kant had observed in *The Conflict of the Faculties* (*Der Streit der Fakultäten*, 1798; see Kant, 1992), that the University was created by the *enactment of an idea*. An objectivation of the Will to Reason as ceded, in principle, from what is *de jure* a metaphysical incipit *a priori* the inscription of being. Or a *fatum* of the time-lessness of Being, the ground and abyss of its infinity. That is, the *principle of reason*. Kant, as only he could, attempted to re-theorise the insights and shortcomings of such a novel idea as the university in an architectonic division of intellectual labour pure and practical. The uni-form system of knowledge designations starts from 'the idea of the whole field of what is presently teachable (*das ganze gegenwärtige Feld der Gelehrsamkeit*)' (Derrida, 1983, p. 6). But the irony is that owing to the 'artificiality' (*Künstliche*) of the institutional architecture 'one would [have to] treat knowledge a little like an industry (*gleichsam fabrikenmässig*)' (Derrida, 1980, p. 5) and be commited to reproducing the rigid partitions of unsurpassable limits marking the separation between disciplines. A development related to the themes of 'profession', 'professionalism' or 'professionalisation', Derrida views its effects as 'regulat[ing] university life [and the ethics of research] according to the supply and demand of the marketplace [not excluding the institution itself] and according to a purely technical idea of competence' (Derrida, 1983, p. 17). Any 'sociology or politology' (ibid., p. 16) policing these borderlines of the Academy—regardless of method (e.g. 'Marxist or neo-Marxist, Weberian or neo-Weberian, Mannheimian, some combination of these or something else entirely', ibid., p. 16)—must respond to the necessity of justifying the value of its own existence and acceptance in relation to the structural logic of the organic whole of the institution. Otherwise, as Derrida explains, it 'never touches upon that which, in themselves, continues to be based on the principle of reason and thus on the essential foundation of the modern university' (ibid., p. 16). Even the most underground thinking—even 'deconstruction'—can be rehabilitated or reappropriated to serve a 'highly traditional politics of knowledge' (ibid., p. 17) if the conditions of exposition ('historical, techno-economic, politico-institutional, and linguistic', ibid., p. 17) are not analysed with a vigilant wariness, a radical suspicion. Rather than encouraging the open harmony of higher and lower level orders of theory and practice, Kant envisions, wants, or presumes, the attempt to separate and compartmentalise interests is the source of the conflict of the faculties itself and an omen of the history of canonical battles, among and within them, for control over the charted and uncharted territory grounding the 'economy and ecology' (ibid., p. 16) of the institution.

In so far as 'no experience in the present allows for an adequate grasp of that present, presentable totality of doctrine, of teachable theory' (ibid., p. 6). Derrida, in rereading these idealist presuppositions of Kant's seminal text on the straining inter-relations of the disciplines, argues that: 'An institution—this is not merely a few walls or some outer structure surrounding, protecting, guaranteeing or restricting the freedom of out work; it is also and already the structure of our interpretation' (Derrida, 1980, p. 22). The ethics of the ground of that edifice of the university is what is being questioned here, along with the responsibility to be taken for it. And who this 'our' *does* or *can* refer to exactly. This is not to aver, as Kant would have it, that philosophy—the faculty from which the 'Great Model of the University' acquires the academic legitimacy of its ideal autonomy—is completely 'outside' and 'above' any hierarchisation of knowledge due to a 'higher' responsibility it claims to answer for/to Reason and Truth. There is another side to it (see Derrida, 1984). Concurrently, philosophy (unlike other disciplines) would also need to be 'inside' and 'below' the structure of the institution, filling out the reason of the lower ground on which its being stands. But what of the originary violence of a *faculty of Right*? Is the 'mystical foundation of its authority' as a legislator of 'Reason' and 'Truth' for the university assuaged by an inverted mirroring of its stature? Could it be?

Even if we choose to believe Kant, there is a minimal security, if any at all, to the tautological notion of 'the essence of knowledge as knowledge of knowledge' (Derrida, 1980, p. 5): the stolid (meta-philosophical) ground of university autonomy. It is 'justified [Derrida stresses] by the axiom stating that scholars alone can judge other scholars' (ibid.). But this still says nothing of academic responsibility. And by this I do not mean the obligation of the institution, a mere husk or shell, a clever figment or apparition of a living entity. It goes deeper. The responsibility I am speaking of is that of the teaching body (*le corps enseignant*), the soul of the university.

On both the personal (I/me) and the communal (us/we) planes of the ethico-juridical strata of the norms of responsibility epistemic or empirical subjectivity submits to, the *first* and *final* law of being is preserved by the ground of reason as the fundamental logic of an institution, *the right of its Right*. But the founding and conserving violence complicit with the historicity of the university does not *wholly* ensnare the inspirited bodies of 'those who teach' either (Derrida, 1983, p. 5). Derrida explains how an uncomplicated philosophy of language is the cause for the ambiguity Kant is blind to:

> Kant defines a university that is as much a safeguard for the most totalitarian of social forms as a place for the most intransigently liberal resistance to any abuse of power, resistance that can be judged in turns as most rigorous or most impotent. In effect, its power is confined to a power-to-think-and-judge, a power-to-say, though not necessarily to say *in public*, since this would involve an *action*, an executive power denied the university. How is the combination of such contradictory evaluations possible for a model of the university? What must be such a model, to lend itself thus to this? I can only sketch out an answer to this enormous question. Presuppositions in the Kantian delimitation could be glimpsed from the very start, but today they have become massively apparent. Kant needs, as he says, to trace between a responsibility concerning truth and a responsibility concerning action, a linear frontier, an indivisible and rigorously uncrossable line. To do so he has to submit language to a particular treatment. Language is an element common to both spheres of responsibility, and one that deprives us of any rigorous distinction between the two spaces that Kant at all costs wanted to dissociate. It is an element that opens a passage to all parasiting and simulacra. (Derrida, 1980, p. 18)

The radical breakdown of the architectonic system and the ethical referencing of knowledge arising from within the Kantian conception of the Law and the Right of Reason's institution becomes perceptible when the philosophical endowment of the limit of its Truth is projected outside of itself 'between [the chain of] language and something other than itself' (Derrida, 1982, p. 216). That, for deconstruction, is but one measure of the injustice of the *universality of the university*. The inconsistency of the supplication of reason to its ground—the accounting of justification itself—surpasses the metaphysical fastidiousness of what Kant presents as an uncorrupted philosophy—of the Idea of Reason—always willing to aid the judgement of a subject 'capable of deciding [as it] tries to limit the effects of confusion, simulacrum, parasiting, equivocality and undecidability produced by language' (Derrida, 1980, p. 18).

Ethics after Idealism: For a new academic responsibility within the university

Wanting to close off the university's inside from its outside (and what this means in a larger context) is a utopian flight of fancy. A fearful withdrawal from an affirmative responsibility to the Other. As is the dream Kant had for a universal language of philosophy uncorrupted by a natural tongue. It constitutes a wish to keep reason pure and its ethics teleological. But the freedom of a decision is characterised not by its end, nor by its salient trajectory. The ability one has to choose freely among manifold options of undecidable and non-indicative possibilities does not demarcate a responsibility abdicated or an obligation ignored; it reveals a responsibility multiplied, an obligation intensified by the power to choose. What I have called the 'ethics of science and/as research' within the university is crystallized through the education of experience manifest of a subjective 'trial of passage' undergone by the researcher in the process of envisioning and responding to the use-value of research outcomes. It is wrought from the difficulty of knowledge and knowing and the academic responsibility incurred by trying to attain and use it responsibly. The responsibility of the decision is in the response to the use-value of research with respect to the Other. A decision here without the possibility of choice, in this sense of achieving an informed claim to truth spurring the application of research, can be no decision at all because it denies responsibility for the Other and therefore denies the Other. And that also implies an ethico-political dimension adducible of the laws of right and Right stemming from the research act. For Derrida—like Kierkegaard before him—the ordeal of decision is an instant of madness, it 'always risks the worst' (Derrida, 1983, p. 19), especially, as concerns us here, in relation to the ethics of research and the grounding of the preconditions of the violence of an existing foundation like the idea of the university's reason for being:

> It is not a matter simply of questions that one *formulates* while submitting oneself, as I am doing here [in the discourse], to the principle of reason, but also of preparing oneself thereby to transform the modes of writing, approaches to pedagogy, the procedures of academic exchange, the relation to languages, to other disciplines, to the institution in general, to its inside and its outside. Those who venture forth along this path, it seems to me, need not set themselves up in opposition to the principle of reason, nor give way to 'irrationalism.' They may continue to assume *within* the university, along with its memory and and tradition, the imperative of professional rigour and competence (ibid., p. 17).

The meta-logic of deconstruction defines the site of the struggle for a new academic responsibility. The double-sided responsibility of its 'to' and 'for' peripatetic aims at a *Verwindung* of the principle of reason that would rearticulate the ethics of science and/as research within the university. After the affirmative ethics of deconstruction, this means a 'going-beyond that is both an acceptance and a deepening' (Vattimo, 1988, p. 172) of reflection on the concepts of ethics, science, and responsibility as Gianni Vattimo has argued, not to get over, overcome, or to distort the principle of these concepts by outbidding them into submission, but to resign the compliance of thought to a rethinking of them (see Gasché, 1994). And thus, to effectuate a change in the thinking of the being of the university and the academic responsibility of our roles in it as researchers and intellectuals. To avoid reproducing the classical architectonic of the Kantian institution, thereby entrenching its effects still further, Derrida asserts, ' "Thought" requires *both* the principle of reason *and* what is beyond the principle of reason, the *arkhè* and an-archy'

(Derrida, 1983, pp. 18–19). With this I agree. The creation of a chance for the future occurs by keeping the memory of the past alive. There must be an archive, a body of knowledge, to work from, for, and against. It is at the inter-spaces of old and new knowledge constructions beyond the grasp of 'meaning' or 'reason' that risks are taken to move beyond what we already know by endeavouring to put the systematicity of what may appear to be grounded or static into motion, play, *kinesis*. The institutional meeting place of a deconstructive ethics and politics would engage the undecidability of interpretative links where a new academic responsibility could be forged between those faculties speaking a constative (theoretical) language of a Kantian type and others who make performative (interventive) statements of an Austinian type. Like a bridge across an abyss of reason.

Notes

1. Derrida, 1983, p. 11. 'The Principle of Reason', we must remember, was written and presented in April of 1983. At the time—the peaking of the 'Cold War' this is a fair description of the homogeneous 'conditionality' of the Western 'nation-states'—most conspicuously exemplified by America and Russia—that according to Derrida were spending in total upwards of 'two million dollars a minute' on the manufacture of armaments alone.
2. Two excellent discussions of the *Collège Internationale de Philosophie* (see Ungar, 1984, pp. 13–26).
3. The open letter was published in the United States in *Substance*, 35 (1982), pp. 80–81.

References

Derrida, J. (1978) Violence and Metaphysics: An essay on the thought of Emmanuel Levinas, trans. A. Bass, in: *Writing and Difference* (Chicago, University of Chicago Press).
Derrida, J. (1980) Mochlos, or the Conflict of the Faculties, in: R. Rand, *Logomachia: The Conflict of the Faculties* (Nebraska, University of Nebraska Press).
Derrida, J. (1982) White Mythology: Metaphor in the Text of Philosophy, trans. A. Bass, in: *Margins of Philosophy* (Chicago, University of Chicago Press).
Derrida, J. (1983) The Principle of Reason: The university in the eyes of its pupils, *Diacritics* (Fall).
Derrida, J. (1984) Languages and Institutions of Philosophy, *Semiotic Inquiry/Recherches Semiotiques*, 4:2, pp. 91–154.
Derrida, J. (1990) Sendoffs, *Yale French Studies*, 77.
Derrida, J. (1992) *The Other Heading: Reflections of Today's Europe*, trans. P.-A. Brault and M. Nass (Bloomington, Indiana University Press).
Derrida, J., Châtelet, F., Faye, J.-P. & Lecourt, D. (1982) *Rapport pour le Collège Internationale de Philosophie* (Paris, Ministre de la Recherche et de l'Industrie).
Gasché, R. (1994) *Inventions of Difference: On Jacques Derrida* (Cambridge, MA, Harvard University Press).
Kant, Immanuel, (1992) *The Conflict of the Faculties*, trans. M. J. Gregor (Nebraska, University of Nebraska Press).
Leitch, V. B. (1986) Research and Education at the Crossroads: A report on the *Collège Internationale de Philosophie*, *Substance*, 50.
Trifonas, P. (1996) The Ends of Pedagogy: From the dialectic of memory to the deconstruction of the institution, *Educational Theory*, 46:3, pp. 303–333.
Trifonas, P. (1998) Reason Unbound: Toward a re-grounding of the metaphysical foundations of the university, *Educational Theory*, 48:3, pp. 395–409.

Trifonas, P. (1999) Deconstructive Psychographies: Ethical discourse and the institution of the university, *Discourse: Studies in the cultural politics of education*, 20:2, pp. 181–199.

Trifonas, P. (2000a) *The Ethics of Writing: Derrida, deconstruction and pedagogy* (Lanham, MD, Rowman & Littlefield), p. 200.

Trifonas, P. (2000b) Technologies of Reason: The grounding of academic responsibility beyond the principle of reason as the metaphysical foundation of the university, in: P. Trifonas (ed.), *Revolutionary Pedagogies: Cultural politics and the discourse of theory* (New York & London, Routledge), pp. 192–237.

Trifonas, P. (2001) Teaching the Other II: *Ethics, writing, community*, in: G. Biesta and D. Égea-Kuehne (eds), *Derrida and Education* (New York & London, Routledge).

Ungar, S. (1984) Philosophy after Philosophy: Debate and reform in France since 1968, *Enclitic*, 8:1–2.

Vattimo, G. (1988) *The End of Modernity: Nihilism and hermeneutics in postmodern culture*, trans. J. R. Snyder (Baltimore, Johns Hopkins University Press).

5
Archiving Derrida

MARLA MORRIS
Georgia Southern University

Archiving Derrida. Impossible. Commentators who attempt to 'frame' Derrida fail. Is he a 'this' or a 'that?' The proper name slips. What is his 'project'? Derrida refuses to tell us what his 'project' is. Commentators who attempt to name his project fail. Some suggest he is, after all, not doing philosophy. Geoffrey Hartman (1981) remarks that Derrida

> is a philosopher who for many is not a philosopher at all but a strange philologist; students of literature often react to him with resentful admiration. His discours de la folie blurs genres or engages in so interminable a mode of analysis that sanity of writing—its indebtedness to evolved conventions, as well as its apparent realism—is threatened. (p. xv)

Sanity and writing are both threatened. What constitutes sane writing? Why not write madly? Reading Derrida and thinking alongside him might demand that one push to the borders of madness, to the borders of zero, to zones of lostness. To be able to tolerate worlds of discomfort and difficulty, sites/cites without foundations, without answers, zones that threaten stability of thought. Pushing back the Cartesian Cogito, one might empty out into a more Buddhist-like state, or float in a dreamlike haze not unlike unconscious meanderings. Still, there is much in the Derridean archive(s) (if one can even think the impossibility of what that might mean) that leaves one hanging on a precipice.

Some cannot go there. Richard Wolin (2000) comments that 'When it is all said and done, even sympathetic commentators and analysts find themselves at a loss to explain what it all means or whether following Derrida's labyrinthine exegesis is ultimately worth the effort' (p. 33). What Wolin misses, I think, is that the Derridean archive begins at a loss or even a lack. But this loss and lack generate more thinking and disturbance than most contemporary philosophy. Philosophical thinking begins in loss and lack. The pause.

Yet, Derrida is not for everyone. Geoffrey Hartman (1981) notes, 'The house that Jack has built, while not a pack of cards, will infuriate those who think books should be solidly constructed, unified, and with an intellectual space defined by clear and resolute boundaries' (p. 2). For me, it is all the more delightful that Derrida challenges even—the book. Like the psyche itself, especially at the edges of experience, reading Derrida's 'books' opens one out toward the leakiness that signals the unconscious (not that the unconscious is one thing, it is radical otherness à la Laplanche, 1999). Derrida (1995d) remarks, 'The philosopher is someone whose desire and ambition are absolutely mad' (p. 139). Derrida's archive, broadly speaking, is brilliantly mad, for he digs exegetically into the most difficult textual material and combines the most unlikely texts—from Socrates to Freud, from postcards to encylopedias, from madness(es) to the archive, from primal scenes to death.

For those who doubt Derrida's philosophical acumen, Geoffrey Bennington (2001) has a few words to say. He argues that the Derridean archive is about death. Death, in other words, is encrypted throughout the corpus of Derrida's texts. This is especially the case in the main text I examine here, *Archive Fever* (1996). The notion of death consumes Derrida in a feverish manner. Bennington (2001) remarks that philosophical thinking should primarily be about this limit experience, it should be about death. Bennington notes

> Today taking something philosophically, then, always involves this more or less hidden [or repressed?] relationship with death, or, by a slightly violent contraction, whatever I take philosophically is death. Death is the only subject of philosophy. ... The philosopher's stone is an inscribed headstone. (p. 3)

The philosopher's stone is death. Bennington remarks that at the end of the day this is what deconstruction is about. Interestingly enough, so too is the psychoanalyst's stone. Freudian or post-Freudian psychoanalytic thinking requires that one cope with notions of the death drive and repetition compulsion—an acting out without remembering—a veering toward zero. Traditionally, however, philosophers seem, at least to me, to be hostile toward psychoanalysis because it puts in question consciousness, reason and the history of epistemology in the Western tradition.

It is interesting that Derrida embraces psychoanalytic thinking not only in *Archive Fever*, but throughout his corpus. Derrida's writings are scattered with encrypted psychoanalytic ways of thinking. Psychoanalytic thought threatens the very 'foundations' of philosophy. Derrida's brilliance is to work within the philosophical tradition while deconstructing its limits. By injecting psychoanalytic ways of thinking into philosophy, Derrida does just this. Derrida (1995c) comments that psychoanalysis teaches us not only about obstacles, repressions and so forth, but it teaches us about ethics and politics as well.

> Psychoanalysis should oblige one to rethink a lot of certainties, for example to reconstruct the whole axiomatics of law, of morality, of 'human rights,' the whole discourse constructed on the agency of the self and of conscious responsibility, the politician's rhetoric, the concept of torture, legal psychiatry and its whole system, and so forth. Not in order to rule out ethical and political statements, on the contrary, for their very future. (p. 127)

Philosophers who argue that Freud was a fraud need to rethink why it is they think this to be the case. Derrida (1996) suggests in *Archive Fever* that this kind of remark is already a repression, already a Freudian impression. The Freudian impression also entails a 'certain madness.' 'A Certain "Madness" Must Watch

Over Thinking' (Derrida, 1995e). Derrida (1987) remarks that we must be open to this certain madness in ourselves. Reason alone is not enough to guide thinking. 'And to let myself be known by madness (it knows me), to leave the door open to it as to Elijah, for a visit whose hour and day it would decide' (pp. 127–128). What is it that opens one to a certain madness? Traces of the unconscious deposited everywhere but nowhere to be found. For Derrida, the unconscious is text. He notes: 'The unconscious text is already a weave of pure traces, difference in which meaning and force are united—a text nowhere present, consisting of archives which are always already transcriptions' (1978, p. 211). The archives of the unconscious are always already 'untranslatable' (1979, p. 77) because of the otherness within language.

At the end of the day, it is impossible to archive the Derridean corpus. When philosophers try to do so they fail. I will not attempt to do that in this paper. Rather, I would like to do a brief study of the 'madness' of Derrida's notion of the archive. The 'madness' of the archives, the slippage of the idea or notion of the archive, reflects the slippage of the unconscious as a site of otherness. This site of otherness left by the Freudian impression in *Archive Fever* will be examined by my own archiving of three Freudian cases of 'madness.' A feverish education is one that is open to the 'madness' of the archive as well as archiving 'madness.' I argue that educators might become more open to the impossibilities/possibilities of thinking otherwise, to allow 'madness' to enter their work as teachers and scholars. It is at the limit experience of madness that one begins to grapple with the other side of otherness.

The 'Madness' of the Archive

Derrida (1996) remarks that grasping the notion of the archive is difficult. As one attempts to articulate what the archive might be, its meaning slips away. What is an archive? This is a difficult philosophical question. My impression is that Derrida is not certain. My impression, too, is that Derrida does not give readers an answer. This is what might infuriate readers. Derrida is not unlike a psychoanalyst. Adam Phillips (2001) comments that 'One of the notoriously annoying things about going to see a psychoanalyst ... is that psychoanalysts don't answer questions' (p. 177). The interminable question of the archive does not have one answer. Yet, Derrida does flesh out some thoughts about what the archive might entail. I do not think Derrida is interested in a literal place of an archive, where someone stands and sifts through microfiche, although, of course, this is part of what archiving is about. Derrida is more interested in the philosophical thinking through of the archive, which is maddening because one really cannot get a grasp of what the archive is.

Derrida states that he is interested in 'modes of archiving' (1990, p. 32). Here he is talking about the book and writing. He remarks that he is interested in studying 'the book/history of writing and history of the book; the model of works and discourses' (1990, p. 32). For Derrida, the book is a symptom of closure, presence and Being. It is the sickness that is Western philosophy. In *Of Grammatology*, Derrida (1976) explains that

> The idea of the book is the idea of totality, finite or infinite, of the
> signifier; this totality of the signifier cannot be a totality, unless a totality
> constituted by the signified preexists it, supervises its inscriptions and its
> signs, and is independent of it in its ideality. The idea of the book, which
> always refers to a natural totality, is profoundly alien to the sense of writing.
> It is the encyclopedic protection of theology and logocentrism against
> the disruption of writing ... (p. 18)

Derrida also remarks that 'The end of linear writing is the end of the book' (1976,
p. 6). Jonathan Culler (1982) notes that traditionally the history of philosophy
signals a wish fantasy of getting rid of writing by getting things right, by doing
close readings, by embracing formalism. Once a philosopher gets it right, he or she
can stop writing about it, whatever it is. Derrida likewise argues that writing is a
threat and the history of Western philosophy has demonstrated the contempt for
writing by arguing that speech is more real, more authentic, more present, closer
to Being. Writing is secondary and trivial and threatening. But there is no getting
rid of writing. The more we write, the more we write, the more that is written.
Commentaries are interminable. Thus, writing commences interminably, especially
when works lend themselves to commentary. Derrida's work on Freud is a good
case in point. Why Freud? Well, Alice Yaeger Kaplan (1990) teaches that some
authors are more archivable than others. 'Some authors yield to archival research
more easily than others. They've written their every word and filled their margins
with speculative notes' (p. 109). Freud's work and work on Freud seem interminable.
I do not think Freudian speculation is due merely to his large corpus of works;
Freudian controversy is the story or archive, if you will, of interest in sexuality,
human relations, eccentricity, refusals, repressions and denials. Derrida (1996)
argues that there is no getting around Freud; even if one refuses to read him, one is
always already affected by his thinking, especially if one is born into the twentieth
or twenty-first century as a European. Freud 'impressed', made an 'impression' on,
European philosophy and education.

By way of 'commencement,' I will announce that like many Derridean notions,
the archive is aporetic, paradoxical and difficult to grasp. As I read *Archive Fever*,
I get the sense that Derrida attempts to say that 'on the one hand' the archive is
thus and so, yet 'on the other hand' the archive gets disrupted, or is disturbed. This
is what is disturbing and maddening. And this is the madness of the notion of the
archive. To make this reading of Derrida readable, or perhaps impossible, I will
first flesh out his 'on the one hand' and then explore his 'on the other hand' as the
workings of the madness of the archive have implications for archiving 'madness.'

It is the 'commencement' that evokes the writing of the archive (Derrida, 1996,
p. 2). The 'arkhe in the physical, historical, or ontological sense, which is to say to
the originary, the first, the principle, the primitive, in short the commencement'
(p. 2) announces the archive. As commencement, as the 'I am here,' 'I have
arrived,' as the 'authoritative' word, the archive emerges (or so it seems). The
function of the archive is what Derrida (1996) terms 'consignation' (p. 31). To
consign is to 'gather together,' to sign, to endorse the 'signature' (p. 5) of the

'proper name' (p. 5). To tell the story, the primal scene, the originary trauma. This originary story gets lodged in a 'domicile' (p. 2) and is kept 'in this domicilation, in this house arrest' (p. 2). The archive is gathered together as a story under house arrest. It gets arrested (perhaps psychologically) by the 'archons' (p. 2), the guardians. This 'single corpus' (p. 3) is kept ('Quiet as its kept', Morrison, 1985, p. 2069). Derrida says that 'In an archive, there should not be any dissociation, any heterogeneity, or secret' (p. 3). But what archives conceal are indeed secrets, omissions, dissociations, transferences, reversals (Morris, 2001).

On the other hand. The secret that gets repressed begins pushing up, splitting, getting dissociated. The archive is disturbed from within its own house. The disturbance appears symptomatically in and through language. One example of this might be Derrida's (1979) discussion of the disturbance as it gets instantiated in the madness of language within Blanchot's work. Maurice Blanchot's 'La Folie du jour,' says Derrida (1979), 'is a story of madness (histoire de la folie), of that madness that consists in seeing the light, vision or visibility from an experience of blindness' (p. 91). There is a certain 'untranslatability' (1979, p. 77) encrypted in the title itself, which 'drives the reader mad' (p. 89). Deconstructing Blanchot's title, Derrida asks if it means 'the madness of today' (p. 89), or 'I went mad' (p. 89), or 'The madness of the day itself' (p. 89). On and on interminably. And yet. It is not simply language itself that is maddening, it is something beside language, it is the parasite, the beside, that which is always nagging at words, at writing, at thinking. Derrida cites Nietzsche in *Ecce Homo* whereby he says 'I am my father who is dead and my mother who is alive' (1979, p. 91). This is not merely a language game or a question of words, it is altogether more serious. This is the language of unconscious traces. Some might suggest it is a symptom of symbiosis, of transference, of unfinished mourning, of splitting, of regression, of dissociation, of madness. The archive, thus, is split always already by the 'untranslatability' (Derrida, 1979, p. 77) of the unconscious. The archive is thus 'disjointed' (Derrida, 1996, p. 29). It is in fact encrypted by heterogeneity and dissociation, splitting off, repression and suppression, says Derrida. I am my dead father. What kind of a statement is this? Whatever it is, it leaves the impression of haunting. In fact, Derrida remarks that the archive is haunted, inscribed, encrypted with 'phantoms.' The return of the repressed, the ghost of Freud, of Banquo, of Hamlet's father, Nietzsche's father, Marley's ghosts and Thomas Wolfe's (1957) 'wind, grieved ghost' (n.p.) haunts the archives.

What haunts the archives is something feverish. It is the death instinct or death drive which drives the archive, says Derrida (1996). The death drive could be interpreted superficially as that limit experience 'that I am going to die' which keeps the archive in motion. Freud's 'superstitions,' that he was always on the verge of dying, kept him writing; Freud writes out of a sense of impending death. 'I have worked hard, am worn out, and am beginning to find the world repulsively disgusting. The superstition that has limited my life to around February 1918 seems downright friendly to me' (1917/1996, p. 249). Of course Freud's superstition was wrong. He died in 1939. But he had this incredible sense of urgency in his work because of his fears and premonitions about death. The death drive might also be interpreted as what is underneath the work of doing justice to the memory of others' deaths or the death of the other. Derrida says that he writes out of a sense of mourning, 'the mourning of mourning' (1995b, p. 49) keeps him writing. What else is mourning about other than death, one's own impending death or the death of another? Derrida (1987) calls autobiographic writing 'Autothanatography' (p. 273). Moreover, Derrida comments that he 'writes also for the dead' (1988, p. 53). Further, he states, 'What discourse does not call up the deceased?' (1997, p. 94). The philosopher's stone is the headstone (Bennington, 2001). Call it the death drive, the death instinct, or something to do with death. Perhaps working on the self is always already work on or around death, one's own mortality. Whatever one calls it, it is the fever of death that keeps the archive moving. Encrypted within the archive is death.

What Freud connected to the death drive, though, is repetition compulsion, an acting out without remembering, a spiraling toward zero. Self-destruction, repeating without recollecting or remembering, repeating the primal scene, the unresolved Oedipal complex, transferring unresolved issues from the family romance to the site of everyone; transferring the father, mother, or both onto others as a form of generalized transference. Derrida (1996), after Freud, notes repetition compulsion keeps the archive alive. If the writer of the archive is working out of repetition compulsion, the archive is alive with all kinds of tranferential relations. The archive is not what it seems. Transference and repetition compulsion is what Derrida terms the 'anarchivic' (1996, p. 10) movement always already at work within the archive. To work through repetition compulsion, one re-peats, re-historicizes, re-makes, forgets. Repetition compulsion is forgetting; one repeats and acts out what one cannot remember. Hence, Derrida writes that 'forgetfulness and the archiviolithic [get injected] into the heart of the monument. Into the "by heart" itself' (pp. 11–12). Writers write without remembering, but keep writing, making 'monuments,' not of brick, but of ash, of 'cinders.' Sometimes these cinders get repressed. Hence, 'the violence of the archive' (Derrida, 1996, p. 7). Perhaps by violence, Derrida suggests an interminable wrestling of eros and thanatos as the archive gets played out through regressions, repressions, suppressions, reversals and so forth against the larger cultural, historical backdrop.

Hence, the politics of the archive comes into play. Repressed archives get concealed but because of slips, of parapraxis, openings, of leaks. The guardians are on holiday. What is encrypted returns and does so in distorted ways, it doubles its strength in the return, but does not mimic exactly or precisely the primal scar. An example of a repressed archive is cited in Derrida's (2001) essay titled 'History of the Lie: Prolegomena', which grapples with repressed archival memory:

> Six Presidents of the French Republic (Auriol, Coty, de Gaulle, Pompidou, Giscard d'Estaing, Mitterrand) had deemed it [the French complicity during the Holocaust] until now neither possible, opportune, necessary, nor even correct, just to stabilize it as a truth of this type. Not one of them believed he was obliged to commit France, the French Nation, the French Republic, with a kind of signature that would have to

assume responsibility for this truth: France guilty of a crime against
humanity. (pp. 76–77)

The archive (of deconstruction) is inextricably tied to ethics and politics (Trifonas,
2000). A repressed archive, or what Derrida calls a lie, returns. And it returns
tenfold. Like a virus that is not fully cured, the repressed comes back in more
distorted forms over time.

Yet, the archive is not about the past, says Derrida (1996), it is about the future.
Archivization is not about historization, it is about something 'to come' which one
does not understand. The 'impression' (p. 29) that remains is interminably a mys-
tery. '[W]e will only know in times to come perhaps [what the archive means, what
impression it leaves]. Not tomorrow but in times to come, or perhaps never' (1996,
p. 36). One of the reasons one cannot know what impression the archive will leave,
is that archives are obscured because of unconscious traces deposited in the text of
the archive. For example, if we talk about the signature, Sigmund Freud, and
attempt to study his life from a biographer's perspective, we might be immediately
struck by the density of material available, but what is particularly striking is what
is missing in the Freudian archive. Louis Breger (2000) points out that Freud
'Destroy[ed]' (Freud, cited in Breger, 2000, p. 1) many of his letters and papers,
thus, 'obscuring the details of his life' (p. 1). Freud wanted to make it difficult, says
Breger, for his biographers. Many of Freud's letters have still not been 'released
from censorship' (Breger, 2000, p. 58). Aha, the secrets. The guardians of the
archive keep the secrets alive!! The more secrets deposited in the archive, the more
suspect the archive becomes. What is concealed and why?

Freud's letters might be considered a form of autobiography. But here, too, the
letters guarantee little understanding of Freud's complicated life history. Derrida
(1995e) remarks that 'The most private autobiography comes to terms with great
transferential figures, who are themselves and themselves plus someone else' (p. 353).
Whose Freud? (Brooks & Woloch, 2000). Freud who? The signature? The trace?
The promise?

The Freudian archive, the Freudian project, is also marked by transferential
relations. Jones's biography of Freud suggests that Ferenczi, according to Freud,
went mad toward the end of his life (Breger, 2000). But according to Judith
DuPont (2000) Freud was wrong, Ferenczi did not go mad, Jones was simply
jealous of Ferenczi's relationship with Freud and wanted to become Freud's
favorite son, even though Freud had much contempt for Jones. DuPont remarks:

> After Ferenczi's death, the correspondence between Freud and Jones
> showed to what extent Freud himself detected a psychotic decom-
> pensation in Ferenczi's scientific approach [perhaps a statement about
> the so-called kissing technique]. Those of us who understand the enormous
> influence that Ferenczi's final articles have today can appreciate how
> wrong Freud was at the time. Jones only accentuated Freud's judgment,
> motivated no doubt by his own convictions, but also perhaps by a little
> jealousy ... (p. xxxviii)

What, indeed, is the jealous archive? The guardians cannot keep watch over jealous emotions and transference. Whatever it is that motivates one to do archival work, i.e. biographies, cannot be separated out from emotions. I do not believe that one chooses a subject matter randomly. The pull toward a person, a book, a writing, a topic, is perhaps part of the repetition compulsion or at least part of an unconscious working through. Alice Yaeger Kaplan (1990) argues that 'only the most extreme emotions can drive people to the drudgery, to the discomfort, of sitting and sifting through dog-eared documents' (p. 104). If one works out of a place of no emotion, this needs to be analyzed. Intellectualization signals repression (Morris, 2001). Intellectual work should be emotional work or the work that is being done will be problematic on all kinds of levels.

Intellectual work of archiving, of writing archives, of creating archives, is done within a system, usually a university system. The university is another kind of archive in itself, a site for the production of intellectual work. If the archive is about the history of writing, one must ask what the system of the university does to the writing and what the institution of the university does to the history of the archive. Derrida is curious about the limits that the university imposes on the working of the archive and on writing in general and he wonders about how to work within the university, how to write the archive within the university while at the same time being limited by the university. Derrida (1995a) writes about his struggles within the university. Since his work is on the edge of disciplinarity, since he draws on philosophy, psychoanalysis and literature, university scholars have difficulty pegging him. Derrida suggests that one is always situated within the institution and yet one might work at the edges of the institution so as not to become what I would call a castrated scholar. To deconstruct the site of the institution of the university is part of the work of archiving.

Unlike Derrida, Adam Phillips (2001) argues that institutions do too much damage to creative thinkers; and in the case of psychoanalysts, he suggests that to do good psychoanalytic work, whether writing or practice, one must leave psychoanalytic institutes. Phillips (2001) argues that 'If there are to be usefully inspiring psychoanalysts in the future ... they must never involve themselves in formal groups—or so-called institutes of psychoanalysis' (p. 111). What institutes do, says Phillips, is attempt to 'purify the dialect of the tribe' (p. xiii). Likewise, the archive, as reflected in scholarly journals, is marked or guarded by the guardians of journal editors, who are, in the field of curriculum studies, for example, mostly white male conservators of tradition. Scholarly writing in the house of the patriarchal archive, as it is guarded mostly by white male conservators, tends toward flattening language, standardizing ideas and erasing anything too quirky. Clipped prose is simply not acceptable in the patriarchal archive. If anything, the patriarchal archive enjoys the style of no style. This is a sign of 'objectivity,' 'clarity,' 'masculinity' and 'truth.' This truth is the lie of the patriarchy. As William F. Pinar (2001) suggests, this kind of archive, this patriarchal archive is suffering from a 'crisis of masculinity.' One would like to escape the system, as Adam Phillips (2001) suggests, but Derrida says that this is impossible. Derrida argues that one cannot step outside the system of the university as a scholar, and if one does one has already begun to normalize one's style, one's ideas. Thus, if scholars are willing to work simultaneously within the institution of the university, yet at the edges of the university, one takes part in the deconstruction of the university, which has always already been taking place. If one works only within the university without working at the edge of that institution one can only become a castrated shadow of oneself.

The question, then, becomes: to whom is the archive (whatever that may mean at this point, books, journals, autobiographies, biographies, the university) directed? Peggy Kamuf (1997) argues that, as against the commonsense understanding of scholars as ivory tower elitists separated from the real world, professors are in fact the most public of all public citizens. Kamuf (1997) states: 'Unlike that of other institutions ... the generation, support, gathering, storage, evaluation, study, presentation, and publishing of publications ... the university is perhaps the most public of all public institutions' (p. 133).

The scholarly archive, thus, is public. It is indeed open to public scrutiny, but Kamuf points out that scholars are constantly being attacked for not being public, hence the pressure to become a 'public' intellectual. Since the general public does not read scholarly monographs, or scholarly journal articles, scholars are not writing for the public, they write for themselves, and that is not 'public' but private. But, as Derrida points out, there is no one public. In a Derridean fashion, Kamuf (1997) argues that one cannot tell who or what the public is 'Since division describes the very possibility of any addressee at all' (p. 160). The archive is not addressed to the public as if the public had a monolithic substance. As Derrida (1998) remarks, the only language he addresses the public in is a 'monolingualism of the other.' The language of the other is encrypted with its own otherness and hence there is no one other, no one public, no one addressee, no one residence, no one designation.

Educational scholars often talk about otherness. The journals in the field of curriculum studies and philosophy of education reflect this trend. But I find that most of the work done on otherness is superficial because scholars do not really want to know what otherness is, probably because they are too afraid of their own otherness within. If we are to understand that the archive opens out toward a public which is a public of others and others are indeed other, it is important to look at least briefly at what eccentric lives are and why educational scholars might be open to these quirky ways of living a life. Is it not interesting if scholars dwell in clipped prose? What does that kind of thinking signify, what might it reflect?

It is interesting to note that, not unlike the discipline of education, psychoanalytic thinkers, too, talk about otherness. But even in a discipline that deals head-on with eccentricity, psychoanalysts tend to squash that which they cannot manage psychologically and this is reflected in their writing. Adam Phillips (2001) points out that 'much psychoanalytic theory which preaches the value of otherness ... should so often be quoting the same limited people' (p. 22). The work of citation is also the work of archiving and archiving is not unrelated to canonization (Kaplan, 1990). Psychoanalytic thinkers and educational scholars, whether consciously or unconsciously, feel the need to repeat, re-cognize, other people's bibliographies for fear of being rejected or not published. Too obscure a bibliography could mean too obscure a career. Obscurities!! My sources are not terribly obscure within perhaps deconstructionist—literary circles or psychoanalytic circles. But within educational discourse, what I am doing in this paper might seem obscure to some of my colleagues in the field of education who are mired in cognition and statistical studies. However, there are a handful of thinkers in curriculum theorizing who have for many years been dealing with psychoanalytic and or Derridean issues (most notably, Pinar, 1975/2001; Britzman, 1998; Trifonas, 2000; Morris, 2001; Pitt, Robertson & Todd, 1998; Appelbaum & Kaplan, 1998; Block, 1997; Grumet, 1988; Atwell-Vasey, 1998; Salvio, 1998). Against the backdrop of the larger field of education though, this number is quite small.

Archiving 'Madness'

One cannot archive madness without grappling with the madness of the archive itself, and since Derrida has taught us about the complexities of the archive and the madness within the archive itself, we can now move on.

Three notably eccentric lives are archived by Freud: the Wolf Man, the Rat Man and Dr. Daniel Paul Schreber. Following Adam Phillips (2001), I want to argue that 'no one is "ill"'' (p. xv); that what psychoanalysis teaches is 'the possibility of [living] an eccentric life' (p. xiii). Also, I do not want to romanticize states of psychosis and or neurosis because they are frightening and sometimes awful and I do not want to equate psychosis and or neurosis with brilliance or madness with brilliance. This commonsense understanding is misguided. I want to discuss otherness as it is archived by Freud. If teachers want to have democratic classrooms and relate to their students in ways that foster democratic discussions, they must grapple with limit experiences of otherness, because some of our students live in these spaces. Otherwise, teachers are clueless.

What I want to do in this limited space is follow, in a cursory fashion, some of Freud's remarks about these three remarkable cases, to open educators to otherness, to the other side of otherness, to the dark side of the moon.

The Wolf Man was terrified by a picture of a wolf in a children's story book. Freud (1963/1993) remarks that 'Whenever he caught sight of this picture he began to scream like a lunatic that he was afraid of the wolf coming and eating him up' (p. 172). The Wolf Man was also terrified of butterflies, beatles, horses and caterpillars. Michael Eigen (1993) teaches us that bugs are especially rich unconscious material. In fact, he calls for what he terms a phenomenology of bugs to better understand what it feels like to be terrified of what is lodged or encrypted in the unconscious. The Wolf Man later transferred his fears of bugs and horses and wolves onto his 'school master' (Freud, 1963/1993, p. 197). And later still, he again transferred his fear of his Latin school master to other school masters. Freud's (1963/1993) passage is worth citing/archiving:

> While he was at his secondary school the Fates provided him with a remarkable opportunity of reviving his wolf phobia. ... The Master who taught him Form Latin was called Wolf. From the first time he felt cowed

by him, and he was once taken severely to task by him for making a stupid mistake in a piece of Latin translation. From that time on he would not get free from a paralysing fear of this master, and it was soon extended to other Masters besides. (p. 197)

Transference is at work in the case of the Wolf Man. From the school master's point of view, however, the Wolf Man might have seemed a bafflement. When students display 'irrational' fears, something is at work in the complicated process of transference. Freud would perhaps call this a negative transference which has nothing at all to do with wolves, horses, bugs, or school masters, but in the case of the Wolf Man, phobias had everything to do with witnessing the primal scene.

When a student acts out, the simplest response from the teacher is to run away from the trouble. One of the reasons teachers might run away might have to do with old folklorish beliefs about 'weirdness.' Denise Jodelet (1989) argues that a common feature around 'madness' is 'the belief in contamination' (p. 21). To avoid someone who is different might be a symptom of denial about one's own 'weirdness.' Jodelet (1989) tells us that in a small French community whereby the mad were integrated with the townspeople, the townspeople typically avoided the 'mad' because of the 'Folklorish belief in the transmission of insanity by the bodily fluids and anything which has been in contact with them' (p. 21). Derrida (1978) points out that contamination issues emerge alongside the proper name. The proper name signifes 'clean, toilet-trained' (1978, p. 183), or 'nonpollution of the subject' (p. 183). Derrida (1978) argues that 'the concept of madness, quite simply, is solidified during the era of the metaphysics of a proper subjectivity' (p. 183).

Foucault (1965/1988) documents/archives ways in which avoidance of contamination via madness gets played out in the historical arena. Early on, the 'mad' were shipped off, then hospitalized, then punished in the most sadistic ways. The mad were put in cages, bound, flogged, displayed for public consumption. Reading Foucault's treatment of 'mental illness,' which highlights sadistic punishment by the psychiatric community, becomes totally numbing after a while. Ironically, Foucault's point is missed because the more sadistic the book becomes, the more uninteresting the subject matter, at least for me. More interesting, though, is his treatment of the 'ship of fools.' The phrase has become so commonplace, sedimented, and sanitized that many do not know to what it referred historically. Foucault remarks, 'It is possible that these ships of fools, which haunted the imagination of the entire early Renaissance, were pilgrimage boats, highly symbolic cargoes of madmen in search of their reason: Some went down to the Rhineland rivers toward Belgium and Gheel ...' (1965/1988, p. 9). I think Foucault's texts on madness important and interesting, but I do not agree with his overall thesis that psychoanalysis is the culprit. I think this thesis quite simplistic. Yes, psychoanalysis is problematic but it is not easily reduced. Dismissing is easier than grappling. Moreover, Derrida rightly points out that for Foucault 'everything transpires as if Foucault knew what "madness" means' (1978, p. 41). I would agree with Derrida that when talking of the Wolf Man and the ship of fools, the Rat Man, or Dr. Schreber, one must not reduce their symptoms to a 'disease' and offer up a 'cure.'

To reduce any complex person to a this or a that is a terribly misguided strategy and ultimately unethical. Derrida (1978) argues that we must remain vigilant against 'psychomedical reduction' (p. 170) and hence 'neutralization' (p. 170) for example of 'poor M. Antonin Artaud' (p. 171). If we say, 'poor Wolf Man' and think we understand him, that we understand the complexities of transferring the primal scene onto his school masters, we are a ship of fools. Of Artaud, Derrida says, he 'absolutely resists ... clinical or critical exegesis' (p. 175). So too the Wolf Man.

At the outset of this paper, I stated that philosophical understanding begins in lack and loss. Here too, psychoanalytic understanding begins in lack and loss. A loss of words perhaps and a lack of understanding, and perhaps a lack that demands space for reflection, not judgment. Perhaps phobias are not as difficult to think through (since many of us have them) as psychotic experience, i.e. Dr. Schreber. I do not know how many of us have actually had psychotic episodes, or anything like them. I do not even venture to guess what these are like. But I can think about them and imagine what they might be like and study them to better understand that I have no grasp of this. As I have argued elsewhere, we must keep these difficult limit experiences difficult (Morris, 2001).

Like the Wolf Man, the Rat Man begins with a lack, but not a lack of rat symbology. Everthing was coming up rats. His father was a 'Spielratte' (Freud, 1963/1993, p. 49). He developed a 'regular rat currency' (p. 52). Freud says that rats can signifiy 'syphilitic infection' (p. 52), 'something uncanny' (p. 53), or become 'symbols of dread' (p. 52). The Rat Man exhibited 'Crazy conduct to which he gave way at one time when he was preparing for an examination—how, after working till far into the night, he used to go and open the front door to his father's ghost, and then look at his genitals in the looking-glass' (Freud, 1963/1993, p. 59). The Rat Man also 'believed in premonitions and in prophetic dreams, he would constantly meet the very person of whom ... he had just been thinking' (Freud, p. 60). Ghosts in the archive. Hamlet's father, I am my dead father (Nietzsche), the ghost of Christmas past, the ghost in a looking-glass darkly, the dark side of the moon. There's someone in my head who isn't me? The ghost of others introjected and blurred. What about this Rat Man? Derrida (1987) remarks, 'yes, I was speaking to you of the Rat Man. Nothing about it has been understood yet, or so I feel' (p. 68). I certainly do not understand the Rat Man.

But the person who is least understandable of the three archived here, and the most interesting, I might add, is the 'crazy' Dr. Schreber. Philip Rieff points out that 'Dr. Daniel Paul Schreber ... was a case Freud never saw. This case is remarkable among all Freud contemplated because the patient was a psychotic, a type Freud never treated' (1963/1993, p. ix). Freud 'psychoanalyzed' a patient who was, in a sense, absent. Analyzing the text of a patient, rather than doing analysis in the flesh, raises some interesting questions for deconstructing texts. If all is text, as Derrida teaches, then analyzing Schreber's memoirs as if Schreber were present would be perfectly legitimate. It is also noteworthy that Freud could not stand to look at people or touch them. That is why he did not look at them face to face when doing analysis. So in a sense the analysand of Freud's analytic scene was absent while present. Her gaze did not meet Freud's. When someone is not looking in your eyes are they present or absent, or is there a kind of absent presence or present absence or are they totally absent? Still, some might argue that analyzing Schreber's text is not the same as analyzing him in the flesh, in person. Would Schreber's analysis by Freud be more real if he had actually been present? Derrida (1976) suggests that speech, Being, presence and voice are not more real than writing. Schreber's memoirs are not derivative of Schreber, of his spoken word; Schreber's memoirs are not secondary to the literal voice of Schreber. Writing is always already in speech, Derrida tells us. Thus, in the case of Schreber, the patient need not be literally present. The reverse is also true for those of us who try to learn from the analyst, Freud. Freud's absence does not matter. Derrida explains: 'the analyst himself, not even his generation, does not need to be "there," in person. He can be all the stronger in not being there. He sends himself—and the postal system forwards' (1987, p. 339).

Schreber's memoirs reveal a psychosis that for the everyday reader makes little sense. If one were to pick up Schreber's memoirs without any background in psychoanalysis, one might think he were writing a fantasy novel. Schreber's (2000) memoirs read strangely: 'Soul-voluptuousness had become so strong that I myself received the impression of a female body, first on my arms and hands, later on my legs, bosom, buttocks and other parts of my body' (p. 163). Schreber talks of 'high-grade voluptuousness' (p. 165). Later he discusses how this 'voluptuousness' gets disturbed. 'If only my voluptuousness were not disturbed' (p. 201). Schreber builds a sort of philosophical system out of voluptuousness. He states quite firmly and with much conviction that

> Voluptuousness is given even to the worm, but it's the Cherub who stands before God. Nevertheless there is an essential difference. Voluptuous enjoyment or Blessedness is granted to souls in perpetuity and as an end in itself. ... An excess of voluptuousness would render man unfit ... (p. 249)

And so on. On and on about voluptuousness. Freud (1963/1993) tells us that Schreber 'believed he was dead and decomposing' (p. 89) and 'he felt he was God's wife' (p. 107). Michael Eigen (1993) tells us that Freud argued that 'psychosis was a fixation and/or regression to primary narcissism (as reflected in megalomania) or to autoeroticism (the loss or extreme fragmentation of the ego)' (p. 45). Eigen (1993) tells us that Wilfred Bion explains psychotic experience as 'deanimating' (p. 67), 'monotonic blankness,' 'as a slippage to zero' (p. 67). Eigen (1993) says psychotic states can be 'terrifying' (pp. 32–33). He explains that

> The psychotic self may approximate moments of absolute fusion and/or isolation. ... The individual lives in a swamp or vacuum. The self becomes sponge-like and spineless, or brittle and rigid. More often the self goes both ways at once and is confused by its mixture of nettle and putty (p. 148).

Archiving madness teaches that there are 'worlds within' (Aswell, 1947) that are not what we think, that the 'world next door' (Peters, 1950) is other. The other is also within and if the archive were to let go of the guardians, one might find somebody at home who is not at home. Eigen (1993) says, 'It is no longer easy to separate madness from sanity, if ever it was' (p. 213). Eigen is not saying that everyone is in fact psychotic. But I do think he is suggesting that limit experiences can be unearthed or lurk somewhere close to home. He says, 'If we are mad, we make ourselves more so by scratching (zeroing or irritating) the terms of our experience' (p. 250). And it is this that schooling militates against. In his early groundbreaking essay titled 'Sanity, Madness and the School,' William F. Pinar (1975/2001) states:

> As many have pointed out, the informing image of young people implicit in American schooling is that children are basically wild, unpredictable beasts who must be tamed and domesticated. Hence they cannot be trusted until they have internalized the values of socially controlled and emotionless adults. (p. 360)

The socialization of wild beasts is disastrous. Schooling erases creativity and exploration of inner worlds. The squashing of emotion, however, returns as the ghost and phantom of the archive.

Beasts, however, can fly up to the sky, beasts can travel inward, beasts can growl and beasts can produce great works of art, beasts can talk of voluptuousness. We have lost the beastly within this sanitized American culture. Call back the beasts. Beasts can be poets. In fact, Adam Phillips (2001) suggests that he wants his patients to become better poets, even though, 'Poets, after all, are not known for their mental health' (p. 11). When Hart Crane committed suicide he ate a full breakfast while on a ship and then threw himself overboard. Sylvia Plath gassed herself to death. Virginia Woolf put rocks in her pockets and walked into the water never to be seen alive again. Gilles Deleuze threw himself out of a window. Ernest Hemingway blasted himself with a shotgun. Kurt Cobain blew his brains out.

Phillips (2001) states that the aim of analysis (and I would add education) is to 'enable the patient to be more like this creative writer, able to make known his fantasies, and find them a source of pleasure, to make the patient the good-enough poet of his own life' (p. 9). Students should be able to be good-enough poets of their own lives too. But to be a good-enough student, one must be beastly and gaze into the looking-glass darkly, trace the other side of the moon. The good-enough professor might dare to be mad about the archive and archive her own madness.

Note

Special thanks to MAD for careful reading and suggestions.

References

Appelbaum, P. & Kaplan, R. (1998) An Other Mathematics: Object relations and the clinical interview, *Journal of Curriculum Theorizing*, 14:2, pp. 35–42.

Aswell, M. L. (1947) *The World Within: Fiction illuminating neuroses of our time* (New York, Whittlesey House, McGraw-Hill Book Company, Inc.).

Atwell-Vasey, W. (1998) *Nourishing Words: Bridging private reading and public teaching* (Albany, NY, State University of New York Press).

Bennington, G. (2001) 'RIP', in: R. Rand (ed.), *Futures: Of Jacques Derrida* (Stanford, Stanford University Press), pp. 1–17.

Block, A. (1997) Finding Lost Articles: The return of curriculum, *Journal of Curriculum Theorizing*, 13:3, pp. 5–12.

Breger, L. (2000) *Freud: Darkness in the midst of vision* (New York, John Wiley & Sons).

Britzman, D. (1998) *Lost Subjects, Contested Objects: Toward a psychoanalytic inquiry of learning* (New York, State University of New York Press).

Brooks, P. & Woloch, A. (eds) (2000) *Whose Freud? The place of psychoanalysis in contemporary culture* (New Haven, Yale University Press).

Culler, J. (1982) *On Deconstruction: Theory and criticism after structuralism* (Ithaca, NY, Cornell University Press).

Derrida, J. (1976) *Of Grammatology*, trans. G. C. Spivak (Baltimore, Johns Hopkins Press).

Derrida, J. (1978) *Writing and Difference*, trans. A. Bass (Chicago, University of Chicago Press).

Derrida, J. (1979) Living On: Border lines, trans. J. Hulbert, in: *Deconstruction and Criticism: Harold Bloom, Paul de Man, Jacques Derrida, Geoffrey Hartman, J. Hillis Miller* (New York, Continuum), pp. 75–176.

Derrida, J. (1987) *The Postcard: From Socrates to Freud and beyond*, trans., A. Bass (Chicago, University of Chicago Press).

Derrida, J. (1988) Rountable on Autobiography, trans. P. Kamuf, in: C. McDonald (ed.), *Texts and Discussions with Jacques Derrida: Otobiography, transference, translation* (Lincoln, University of Nebraska Press), pp. 39–89.

Derrida, J. (1990) Sendoffs, in: E. S. Burt & J. Vanpee (eds), *Yale French Studies Number 77 Reading the Archive: On texts and institutions* (New Haven, Yale University Press), pp. 7–43.

Derrida, J. (1995a) *Between Brackets I*, trans. P. Kamuf *et al.*, in: E. Weber (ed.), *Points ... Interviews, 1974–1994* (Stanford, Stanford University Press), pp. 5–29.

Derrida, J. (1995b) 'Ja, in the faux-bond II', trans. P. Kamuf *et al.*, in: E. Weber (ed.), *Points ... Interviews, 1974–1994* (Stanford, Stanford University Press), pp. 30–77.

Derrida, J. (1995c) 'Unsealing ("The Old New Language")', trans. P. Kamuf *et al.*, in: E. Weber (ed.), *Points ... Interviews, 1974–1994* (Stanford, Stanford University Press), pp. 115–131.

Derrida, J. (1995d) 'Dialanguages', trans. P. Kamuf *et al.*, in: E. Weber (ed.), *Points ... Interviews, 1974–1994* (Stanford, Stanford University Press), pp. 132–155.

Derrida, J. (1995e) 'A Certain "Madness" Must Watch Over Thinking', trans. P. Kamuf *et al.*, in: E. Weber (ed.), *Points ... Interviews, 1974–1994* (Stanford, Stanford University Press), pp. 339–364.

Derrida, J. (1996) *Archive Fever: A Freudian impression*, trans. E. Prenowitz (Chicago, University of Chicago Press).

Derrida, J. (1997) *Politics of Friendship*, trans. G. Collins (New York, Verso).

Derrida, J. (1998) *Monolingualism of the Other; or, the prosthesis of origin*, trans. P. Mensah (Stanford, CA, Stanford University Press).

Derrida, J. (2000) *Of Hospitality: Anne Dufourmantelle invites Jacques Derrida to respond*, trans. R. Bowlby (Stanford, Stanford University Press).

Derrida, J. (2001) History of the Lie: Prolegomena, trans. P. Kamuf, in: R. Rand (ed.), *Futures: Of Jacques Derrida* (Stanford, Stanford University Press), pp. 65–98.

Dupont, J. (2000) Introduction, in: E. Falzeder & E. Brabant with P. Giampier-Deutsch (eds), *The Correspondence of Sigmund Freud and Sandor Ferenczi*, vol. 3, *1920–1933*, trans., P. T. Hoffer (Cambridge, MA, Belknap Press of Harvard University Press), pp. xvii–xliv.

Eigen, M. (1993) *The Psychotic Core* (Northvale, NJ, Jason Aronson Inc.).

Foucault, M. (1965/1988) *Madness and Civilization: A history of insanity in the age of reason* (New York, Vintage).

Freud, S. (1917/1996) Letter no. 715, November 1917, in: E. Falzeder & E. Brabrant with P. Giampieri-Deutsch (eds), *The Correspondence of Sigmund Freud and Sandor Ferenczi* vol. 2, *1914–1919* (Cambridge, MA, Belknap Press of Harvard University Press), pp. 249–250.

Freud, S. (1963/1993) *Three Case Histories* (New York, A Touchstone Book, Simon & Schuster).

Grumet, M. (1988) *Bitter Milk: Women and teaching* (Amherst, University of Massachusetts Press).

Hartman, G. H. (1981) *Saving the Text: Literature, Derrida, philosophy* (Baltimore, Johns Hopkins University Press).

Jodelet, D. (1989) *Madness and Social Representations: Living with the mad in one French community*, trans. T. Pownall (Berkeley, University of California Press).

Kamuf, P. (1997) *The Division of Literature: Or the university in deconstruction* (Chicago, University of Chicago Press).

Kaplan, A. Y. (1990) Working in the Archives, in: E. S. Burt & J. Vanpee (eds), *Yale French Studies Number 77 Reading the Archive: On texts and institutions* (New Haven, Yale University Press), pp. 103–116.

Laplanche, J. (1999) *Essays on Otherness* (New York, Routledge).

Morris, M. (2001) *Curriculum and the Holocaust: Competing sites of memory and representation* (Mahwah, NJ, Lawrence Erlbaum & Associates Publishers).

Morrison, T. (1985) The Bluest Eye, in: S. Gilbert & S. Subar (eds), *The Norton Anthology of Literature by Women* (New York, W. W. Norton), pp. 2068–2184.

Peters, F. (1950) *The World Next Door* (London, Victor Gollancz Ltd.).

Phillips, A. (2001) *Promises, Promises: Essays on psychoanalysis and literature* (New York, Basic Books).

Pinar, W. (1975/2001) Sanity, Madness and the School, in: W. Pinar (ed.), *Curriculum Studies: The reconceptualization* (New York, Educator's International Press, Inc.), pp. 359–383.

Pinar, W. (2001) *The Gender of Racial Politics and Violence in America: Lynching, prison rape, and the crisis of masculinity* (New York, Peter Lang).

Pitt, A., Robertson, J. & Todd, S. (1998) Psychoanalytic Encounters: Putting pedagogy on the couch, *Journal of Curriculum Theorizing*, 14:2, pp. 2–7.

Rieff, P. (1963/1993) Introduction, in: *Freud's Three Case Histories* (New York, A Touchstone Book, Simon & Schuster), pp. vii–xi.

Salvio, P. (1998) The Teacher/Scholar as Melancholic: Excavating scholars and pedagogic (s)crypts in fugitive pieces, in: *Journal of Curriculum Theorizing*, 14:2, pp. 15–23.

Schreber, D. P. (2000) *Memoirs of my Nervous Illness*, trans. I. Macalpine & R. A. Hunter (New York, New York Review Books).

Trifonas, P. (2000) *The Ethics of Writing: Derrida, deconstruction, and pedagogy* (New York, Rowman & Littlefield).

Wolfe, T. (1957) *Look Homeward, Angel: The story of the buried life* (New York, Collier Books, Macmillan Publishing Company).

Wolin, R. (2000) The Grandeur and Twilight of French Philosophical Radicalism, in: C. Flood & N. Hewlett (eds), *Currents in Contemporary French Intellectual Life* (New York, St. Martin's Press).

6

Derrida, Pedagogy and the Calculation of the Subject

MICHAEL A. PETERS
University of Glasgow

> The assumption of one single subject is perhaps unnecessary; perhaps it is just as permissible to assume a multiplicity of subject, whose interaction and struggle is the basis of our thought and our consciousness in general? A kind of aristocracy of 'cells' in which domination resides? To be sure, an aristocracy of equals, used to ruling jointly and understanding how to command?
> *My hypothesis*: The subject as multiplicity.
>
> —Friedrich Nietzsche[1]

> I believe that at a certain level both of experience and of philosophical and scientific discourse, one cannot get along without the notion of the subject. It is a question of knowing where it comes from and how it functions.
>
> —Jacques Derrida[2]

Introduction

Luc Ferry and Alain Renaut argue that 'the philosophy of 68' eliminates and leaves no room for a positive rehabilitation of human agency necessary for a workable notion of democracy. In their Preface to the English Translation of *La pensée 68*, Ferry and Renaut (1990a, p. xvi), refer to the philosophy of the sixties as a 'Nietzschean-Heideggerian' antihumanism which is structurally incapable of taking up the promises of the democratic project inherent in modernity. Their criticisms are specifically aimed at Derrida and are intended as a path back to a form of humanism, liberalism and individualism (the doctrine of human rights) which they think can sustain a notion of political agency required for democracy.

Derrida provides us with resources for understanding and responding to these criticisms. He denies a simple-minded nihilism as it applies to the subject, to notions of political agency and to the Idea of democracy and he argues that the anti-Nietzschean polemical attack on the critique of the subject is misplaced; that poststructuralism never 'liquidated' the subject but rather rehabilitated it, decentred it and repositioned it, in all its historico-cultural complexity. As he argues: 'There has never been The Subject for anyone ... The subject is a fable ... but to concentrate on the elements of speech and *conventional* fiction that such a fable presupposes is not to stop taking it seriously (it is the serious itself)' (Derrida, 1995a, p. 264). This paper explores these issues in relation to the project for a critical pedagogy.

Derrida, Humanism and Deconstruction

The American reception of deconstruction[3] and the influential formulation of 'poststructuralism' in the English-speaking world quickly became institutionalised from the point at which Derrida delivered his essay 'Structure, Sign and Play in the Discourse of the Human Sciences' to the International Colloquium on Critical Languages and the Sciences of Man at Johns Hopkins University in October 1966. Richard Macksey and Eugenio Donato (1970, p. x) described the conference as 'the first time in the United States that structuralist thought had been considered as a cross-disciplinary phenomenon'. Even before the conclusion of the conference, there were clear signs that the ruling transdisciplinary paradigm of structuralism had been superseded, yet only a paragraph in Macksey's 'Concluding Remarks' signalled the importance of Derrida's 'radical reappraisals of our [structuralist] assumptions' (p. 320).

In the now classic essay 'Structure, Sign and Play', Derrida (1978b, pp. 279–280) questioned the 'structurality of structure' or notion of 'center' which, he argued, has served to limit the play of structure:

> the entire history of the concept of structure ... must be thought of as a series of substitutions of center for center, as a linked chain of determinations of the center. Successively, and in a regulated fashion, the center receives different forms or names. The history of metaphysics, like the history of the West, is the history of these metaphors and metonymies. Its matrix ... is the determination of being as *presence* in all senses of this word. It could be shown that all the names related to fundamentals, to principles, or to the center have always designated an invariable presence—*eidos, arche, telos, energeia, ousia* (essence, existence, substance, subject) *aletheia*, transcendentality, consciousness, God, man, and so forth.

In this one paragraph Derrida both called into question the previous decade of French structuralism and intimated the directions of his own intellectual ambitions. The decade of French structuralism, beginning with Claude Lévi-Strauss's *Anthropologie structurale* (1958), had its complex cultural prehistory in Nietzsche's critique of modernity, in the development of European structural linguistics, and in early twentieth-century modernism, especially formalism and futurism as it took form in both pre-revolutionary Russia and Italy.[4]

The 'decentering' of structure, of the transcendental signified, and of the *sovereign* subject, Derrida suggests—naming his sources of inspiration—can be found in the Nietzschean critique of metaphysics and, especially, of the concepts of Being and truth, in the Freudian critique of self-presence, as he says, 'the critique of consciousness, of the subject, of self-identity and of self-proximity or self-possession' (1978b, p. 280), and, more radically, in the Heideggerean destruction of metaphysics, 'of the determination of Being as presence' (ibid.). In the body of the essay, Derrida considers the theme of 'decentering' in relation to Lévi-Strauss's ethnology and concludes by distinguishing two interpretations of structure. One, Hegelian in origin and exemplified in Lévi-Strauss's work, he argues, 'dreams of deciphering a truth or an origin which escapes play and the order of the sign' and seeks the 'inspiration of a new humanism'. The other, 'which is no longer turned toward the origin, affirms play and tries to pass beyond man and humanism' (Derrida, 1978b, p. 292).

In another well-known essay, 'The Ends of Man', given as a lecture at an international colloquium in New York two years later (i.e. 1968), Derrida (1982, p. 114) addresses himself to the question 'Where is France, as concerns man?' and he provides an account that interprets the dominant motif of post-war French philosophy as a philosophical humanism authorised by anthropologistic readings of Hegel, Marx and Heidegger. Sartre's 'monstrous translation' (ibid., p. 115) of Heidegger's *Dasein* legitimated an existentialist humanism, and even the critique of humanism, itself a major current of French thought in the post-war era, presented itself more as an amalgamation of Hegel, Husserl and Heidegger with the old metaphysical humanism. Derrida argues: 'the history of the concept man is never examined. Everything occurs as if the sign "man" had no origin, no historical, cultural, or linguistic limit' (p. 116). This statement gives a strong indication as to Derrida's own motivations and directions: a movement towards an ever clearer specification of the subject in historical, cultural and linguistic terms and an excavation of the history of the subject.[5]

Derrida reconsiders the *relève* of man in the thought of Hegel, Husserl and Heidegger to demonstrate that in each case there is a clear critique of anthropologism. In particular, Heidegger's thought is guided by the double motif of being as presence and of the proximity of being to the essence of man (p. 128). He suggests that if we are not simply to restore the ordering of the system by recourse to humanist concepts or to destroy meaning, we face two strategic choices: 'To attempt an exit and a deconstruction without changing terrain, by repeating what is implicit in the founding concepts and the original problematic', and: 'To decide to change terrain, in a discontinuous and irruptive fashion, brutally placing oneself outside, and by affirming an absolute break and difference' (p. 135). And he says, in an oft-quoted remark: 'A new writing must weave and interlace these two motifs of deconstruction. Which amounts to saying that one must speak several languages and produce several texts at once' (ibid.). What we need to 'change the terrain', he claims, finally quoting Nietzsche, 'is a change of "style"; and if there is style, Nietzsche reminded us it must be *plural*' (ibid.).[6]

The relation of both Derrida and deconstruction to pedagogy is as clear as it is fundamental: Derridean philosophy offers an active interpretation, resistance and re-evaluation of humanist pedagogy, of forms of pedagogy based on the sovereign subject—which is to say, the predominant forms of pedagogy existing today that structure our pedagogical institutions, theories and practices. I shall argue that the question of pedagogy is never far from Derrida's concerns; that when he poses the question of style,[7] of new styles of writing and thinking, he is engaged in rethinking traditional humanist pedagogical practices and the founding principles of our educational institutions. This is most straightforwardly the case with applied forms of deconstruction in its relation to pedagogy and Derrida's investigations into the nature of writing as *différance*,[8] such as the deconstruction of the authorial-authoritarian subject.[9] It is the case in Derrida's questioning of the politics and unity of the proper name (see Derrida, 1985). It is also the case in personal or autobiographical terms, where he has deliberated over the *form* of 'philosophical discourse'—its 'modes of composition, its rhetoric, its metaphors, its language, its fictions'—to investigate the ways in which the institutional authority of academic philosophy, and the autonomy it claims, rests upon a 'disavowal with relation to its own language' (Derrida, 1995c, p. 218).[10]

Derrida has never disowned the subject or its relevance either to philosophical or scientific discourse. He has, however, radically questioned the sovereign subject and the philosophical tradition of consciousness that left its indelible imprint on a variety of post-war humanisms. Inspired by Nietzsche and Heidegger, and befriended by Levinas, Derrida has interrogated the humanist construction of the sovereign subject—its genealogy and its authorial functions—in his attempt to develop a science of writing which both deconstructs and moves beyond 'man' as the full presence of consciousness in being. His work has been misinterpreted by those christening themselves anti-Nietzscheans who claim that Derrida (and poststructuralism in general) has 'liquidated' or 'eliminated' the subject and, therefore, endangered agency and posed a consequent threat to a workable notion of democracy.

In the next section, I briefly review the French anti-Nietzscheanism exemplified best by the 'neo-liberals' Luc Ferry and Alain Renaut. Ferry and Renaut argue that 'the philosophy of 68' eliminates and leaves no room for a positive rehabilitation of human agency necessary for a workable notion of democracy.

In the final section, I elaborate the way Derrida provides us with resources for understanding and responding to Ferry and Renaut's criticisms. He denies a simple-minded nihilism as it applies to the subject, to notions of political agency and to the Idea of democracy, and he argues that the anti-Nietzschean polemical attack on the critique of the subject is misplaced; that poststructuralism never 'liquidated' the subject but rather rehabilitated it, decentred it, repositioned and resituated it, in all its historico-cultural and linguistic complexity.

French Anti-Nietzscheanism

Luc Ferry and Alain Renaut published *La Pensée 68* in 1985, poorly translated into the English title as *French Philosophy of the Sixties: An essay on antihumanism* (1990a). In the Preface to the English translation, Ferry and Renaut maintain that French intellectual history since World War II has been dominated by 'a critique of the modern world and the values of formal democracy' (p. xi) inspired by Marx and Heidegger which resulted in a common rejection of humanism. They claim that 'Nietzschean-Heideggerianism' dates the advent of modern humanism from Descartes rather than from the rise of capitalism, and works to 'deconstruct' the subject defined as conscience and will, as 'the author of his acts and ideas' (p. xii). In their description of the trajectory of French post-war thought, they assert that the critique of modern rationality was intimately bound up with the critique of the subject: Marxism had interrogated the universalism of the Enlightenment, based upon claims of the emancipation of man, in the light of Eurocentrism and European colonialism. When Marxism collapsed, the Heideggerian critique took over. They argue, 'the retreat of Marxism has made the presence of Heideggerianism in France more and more visible' (p. xv) and that what happened to Marxism in the 1970s is happening to Heidegger today. In relation to both Marxism and Heideggerianism they summarise their position thus:

> *Whether conducted in the name of a radiant future or a traditionalist reaction, the total critique of the modern world, because it is necessarily an antihumanism that leads inevitably to seeing in the democratic project, for example, in human rights, the prototype of ideology or the metaphysical illusion, is structurally incapable of taking up, except insincerely and seemingly in spite of itself, the promises that are also those of modernity.* (p. xvi, emphasis in the original)

They claim that in their philosophical paradigm—what we can describe as a French neo-liberalism (see Lilla, 1994)—it is necessary 'to grant a minimum of legitimacy to a reference to the subject which is inherent in democratic thought' (p. xvi) and to bypass the confusion between metaphysics and humanism. It is, they claim, after Marx, Nietzsche, Freud and Heidegger, today more than anything 'a question of rethinking ... the question of the subject' (p. xvi).

The antihumanism of French philosophy of the '68 period is tracked out by reference to Derrida's 'The Ends of Man', Foucault's declaration in *The Order of Things* of 'the death of man', and Lyotard's scepticism of anthropologism. Antihumanism holds that 'The autonomy of the subject is an illusion' (p. xxiii) and the problem that now confronts us, Ferry and Renaut suggest, 'consists of searching for conditions for what a *nonmetaphysical humanism* might be' which involves 'conferring a coherent philosophical status on the promise of freedom contained in the requirements of humanism' (p. xxviii). Ferry and Renaut wish to invent a form of modern humanism that is not metaphysical and permits the ascription of universal moral and political judgements and rights without further appeals to essentialist notions of human nature.

In this first attempt, Ferry and Renaut dissipate much of their energies by criticising the Nietzschean-Hedeggerianism. While they legitimately question the Heideggerian critique of subjectivity—the meaning of the 'metaphysics of subjectivity'—and inquire as to what can replace the metaphysical subject after its deconstruction (see p. 212), there are more rhetorical (and less savoury) elements in their attack, which seek to damn Derrida and deconstruction by association with Heidegger's Nazism or Nietzsche's 'irrationalism' and 'illiberalism'.[11] These rhetorical moves aside, there is little sustained engagement with Derrida's texts and their work seems excessively negative or mired in critique, without positively identifying, beyond the most schematic form, in what 'modern humanism' might consist. For instance, toward the end of their book, they argue that 'It does not follow that, having established that man is not really ... autonomous ... one has to go to the extreme of withdrawing all meaning and function ... from the Ideal of autonomy' (p. 211). Or, again, in the conclusion, they indicate that the critique of humanism and of the subject has revealed a 'surprising' simplicity, suggesting that a *history of the subject* still has yet to be written.

As Mark Lilla (1994, pp. 19–20), comments in respect to Ferry and Renaut,

> what they mean by the 'subject' is often obscured in their writings, which up to now have mainly been critical and directed against their adversaries. They have yet to develop their own theory of subjectivity or respond to the objections that all such theories inevitably confront. Still it is clear what they wish such a theory of subjectivity to undergird: a new defense of universal, rational norms in morals and politics, and especially a defense of human rights.

Lilla clarifies that 'such a defense would not be based upon the notion of an isolated individual as possessor of rights and therefore would not be compatible with classical liberalism' (p. 20). Instead, they appeal to a French republicanism that is to be articulated through a new humanism. To date this project has remained entirely programmatic, schematic, and its content has been unfulfilled.[12]

The sorts of criticisms articulated by Ferry and Renaut represent a wider set of criticisms against Derrida and, more broadly, poststructuralism for its theoretical antihumanism and its alleged lack of a subject that can provide either for a notion of political agency and resistance or for the ascription of human rights and the workability of democracy. Indeed, strangely it is on the basis of this generalised criticism that liberals of all persuasions—old-fashioned, feminists, social democrats and neo-liberals—and humanist or disaffected structuralist Marxists and communitarians join hands. This new alliance can be given the generic term 'anti-Nietzscheans'. It is, perhaps, most obvious in the work of Ferry and Renaut (1991), who in the early 1990s published a collection of essays with the title *Pourquoi nous ne sommes pas nietzschéens*, including essays by Vincent Descombes, Alain Boyer, and Philippe Raynaud, among others. Yet it is also clear in the more general attack mounted against Derrida by Barry Smith, the editor of *The Monist* and the inaugurator of the infamous letter that sparked what Derrida called 'the Cambridge Affair'.[13] In the Foreword to a selection of essays edited by Smith (1994) for instance, he claims that the present ills facing American academic life are due directly to Foucault, Derrida, Lyotard and others:

> Many current developments in American academic life—multiculturalism, 'political correctness', the growth of critical theory, rhetoric and hermeneutics, the crisis of scholarship in many humanities departments— have been closely associated with, and indeed, inspired by, the work of European philosophers such as Foucault, Derrida, Lyotard and others. In Europe itself, in contrast, the influence of these philosophers is restricted to a small coterie, and their ideas have certainly contributed to none of the wide-ranging social and institutional changes we are currently witnessing in some corner of American academia.

This set of extraordinary claims are advanced without evidence of any kind; they are, after all, empirical statements rather than analytic ones, and therefore, in terms Smith would accept, the establishment of their 'truth' would necessarily require some historical evidence and analysis.

In the Smith (1994) collection mentioned above, Dallas Willard (1994, p. 15), attempting to address the question of causation implied in Smith's assertions, concludes that to suppose that deconstructionism is *the* cause of the university crisis is a misdiagnosis. Yet he reiterates the charge in Smith's letter that deconstruction is not a *method* of thought. These are general attacks that do not proceed from a direct criticism of the Nietzscheanism assumed, often unproblematically, to exist as a source and inspiration for Derrida and to account for an anti-liberalism in Derrida's thought (and that of other poststructuralists). The essay by Pascal Engel (1994), 'The Decline and Fall of French Nietzscheo-Structuralism', is a clearer example that echoes many of the criticisms raised by Ferry and Renaut. Engel (1994, pp. 36–37, n. 3) distinguishes between what he calls Heideggero-Nietzscheanism (Derrida) and Metaphysical-Nietzscheanism (Deleuze), and formulates his criticisms in terms of a series of theses said to be the basis of Nietzscheo-Structuralism: there is no such thing as meaning, truth, epistemology (theses 1, 3, 4); nothing exists but forces (thesis 2); consciousness and subjectivity are just effects (of affects) (thesis 5); philosophy creates concepts (thesis 6). Engel (1994, p. 34) comments upon the 'catastrophic consequences in political philosophy' of entertaining these theses (as if Deleuze or Derrida actually holds such crudely stated theses).

The new liberal alliance is also strongly evidenced in a recent essay by Charles Taylor (1994) on multiculturalism contributed to a collection edited by Amy Gutmann (1994), including Jürgen Habermas, K. Anthony Appiah, Susan Wolf, Michael Walzer and others. Taylor, for instance, makes casual and offhand remarks concerning 'neo-Nietzscheans', at one point referring to 'subjectivist, half-baked neo-Nietzschean theories' (1994, p. 70). He mentions Derrida and Foucault only once and then without reference to specific texts and in derogatory terms.[14] Taylor argues that citizenship cannot be regarded as a basis for universal identity as people are both unique, self-creating individuals and bearers of culture. Both qualifications could easily be given a Nietzschean perspective, and, indeed, the question of cultural difference has been most thoroughly theorised, one might argue, by Derrida and a host of other poststructuralists (for example, Foucault on micropractices, Lyotard on the *differend*, Deleuze on repetition and difference).

Derrida, for instance, constitutes an important place in the history of the subject when he invents the concept of *différance* and plots the linguistic limit of the subject. *Différance*, as Derrida (1981, pp. 8–9) remarks, as both the common root of all the positional concepts marking our language and the condition for all signification, refers not only to the 'movement that consists in deferring by means of delay, delegation, reprieve, referral, detour, postponement, reserving' but also and finally to 'the unfolding of difference', of the ontico-ontological difference, which Heidegger named as the difference between Being and beings.

Amy Gutmann (1994, p. 13) characterises the concern for *cultural* difference and for the public recognition of particular cultures within liberal democracies as one which is forever counterbalanced by the concern for the protection of universal rights, and she translates the issue into the educational sphere as a dispute over the core curriculum and the content of courses when she sets up the debate in terms of the 'essentialists' and the 'deconstructionists'. Gutmann (ibid., pp. 13–14) suggests that the 'deconstructionists' argue:

> That to preserve the core by excluding contributions by women, African-Americans, Hispanics, Asians, and Native Americans as if the classical canon were sacred, unchanging, and unchangeable would be to denigrate the identities of members of these previously excluded groups and to close off Western civilization from the influences of unorthodox and challenging ideas for the sake of perpetuating sexism, racism, Eurocentrism, close-mindedness, the tyranny of truth (with a capital 'T'), and a host of related intellectual and political evils.

To construct the debate in this way as one between the opposite poles of essentialism and deconstructionism, allows Gutmann to safely impugn both and to come out on the side of liberal democracy. The debate over the core or multicultural curriculum is largely a reflection over the philosophy of the subject: essentialist or deconstructionist? There are a number of buried premises in the argument concerning the liberal theory of education and schooling, the education of reason, the shaping of selves and so on. Gutmann does not make these theoretical connections. Whether she is kind to essentialists I will leave for others to judge. Her take on deconstructionists follows an analogous form to the problem of agency argument: 'deconstructionists erect a different obstacle to liberal democracy when they deny the desirability of shared intellectual standards, which scholars and students might use to evaluate our common education'; 'they [deconstructionists] view common standards as masks for the will to political power of dominant, hegemonic groups' (p. 18). Gutmann asserts that such an argument is self-undermining, both logically and practically, for deconstructionism itself reflects the will to power of deconstructionists. Her quarrel with deconstructionism is that, first, 'it denies *a priori* any reasonable answers to fundamental questions', and, second, 'it reduces everything to an exercise of political power' (p. 20).

The difficulty is that Gutmann 'deconstructionists' are faceless; she never mentions Derrida or any theorist in association with deconstructionism. In other words, she sets up a straw man deconstructionism, which alleviates her of the scholarly *responsibility* to read or refer to specific texts, only to fiercely knock it down in the name of liberal democracy. We are entitled, for instance, to ask Gutmann: can Foucault really be considered a 'deconstructionist'? Is the 'will to power' a motivating concept in Derridean deconstruction or Foucauldian genealogy? Where does Derrida explicitly address the theme of ethnocentrism and what does he say concerning it? Gutmann has homogenised the differences between those she calls 'deconstructionists' and, while appropriating the term deconstructionism, she has ignored any reference at all to Derrida's work. If Gutmann had investigated Derrida's work she might have discovered that ethnocentrism and phallocentrism are seen to accompany the logocentrism that defines historically the attempt in the West to determine being as presence, and that Nietzsche's influence, in Derrida's eyes, has been to free the signifier from the logos.[15]

The anti-Nietzscheanism, perhaps, reached its peak in the early 1990s with Ferry and Renaut's (1991) *Pourquoi nous ne sommes pas nietzschéens*. In the Preface to the 1992 French edition, Ferry and Renaut (1997, pp. vii–viii) suggest that an appropriate re-titling of the collection of essays might be 'To think Nietzsche against Nietzsche', for they identify Nietzsche as the 'inventor of the "genealogy"', the thinker, above all, who inspired the so-called master thinkers of the sixties, who, standing in the shadows of Nietzsche, believed that they too could philosophise with a hammer, smashing the last idols of metaphysics and thereby move beyond humanism. Yet, while they assert that 'today nobody believes in Absolute Knowledge, in the meaning of history, or in the transparency of the Subject' (presumably the *thinking* of Nietzsche), it is also the case that 'philosophy is not condemned to infinite deconstruction' (the thinking of Nietzsche *against* Nietzsche). They continue: 'philosophy renews the ancestral desire for rationality, which the relativism of the modes of thought of difference invited us, too facilely, to renounce'.

Only Vincent Descombes's (1997) essay deals with 'Nietzsche's French Moment' and Descombes's analysis focuses upon Foucault and Deleuze to the exclusion of Derrida. Descombes, generalising to poststructuralism (an 'unnatural alliance' of Nietzscheanism with orthodox structuralism) suggests that Nietzscheanism introduces no new principles apart from those of the 'modern project' and its 'critique of consciousness doesn't go beyond Cartesian mind philosophy' (p. 90). As he says, 'The superior individual is inconceivable outside the idealist philosophy of autonomy' (p. 90).

Ferry and Renaut (1997) bypasses the so-called master thinkers, or any one of them, to concentrate on Nietzsche in relation to the question of democracy. They distinguish two attitudes to democracy: the development or enlargement of the model of argumentative deliberation in either its theoretical or its practical dimensions (Habermas, Apel, Rawls); and the investigation of the possibility of the emergence of a contemporary analogue to a traditional universe through the development of the critique of democratic modernity (Strauss, MacInyre and the 'communitarians'—Taylor, Sandel etc.). Nietzsche's case is interesting, they argue, especially in terms of critically investigating the neo-traditionalist path because he articulates the critique of democratic modernity (and the argumentative foundation of democratic norms) while rejecting the neo-traditionalist possibility of a contemporary analogue of tradition, in an age characterised by the death of God. This is an interesting and productive essay but one which hardly touches Derrida or Derrida's Nietzsche.[16]

Derrida's Response: The calculation of the subject[17]

I shall argue that the anti-Nietzschean polemical attack on the critique of the subject is misplaced, for poststructuralism never 'liquidated' the subject but rather rehabilitated it, decentred it and repositioned it, in all its historico-cultural complexity. While Ferry and Renaut talk of returning to the question of the subject, their critique of poststructuralism and their 'non-metaphysical humanism' singularly lacks any resources for doing so. There is in Ferry and Renaut's work nothing that might suggest a reworking of the question of the subject in any guise except an innocent, historically naive and unproblematic return to a (neo-liberal) human agency.

Jean-Luc Nancy (1991, p. 3) comments in his Introduction to *Who Comes After the Subject?*:

> I did not send my question ('Who comes after the subject?') to those who would find no validity in it, to those for whom it is on the contrary more important to denounce its presuppositions and to return, as though nothing had happened, to a style of thinking that we might simply call humanist, even where it tries to complicate the traditional way of thinking about the human subject.

For Nancy, the contributors (including, Deleuze, Derrida, Blanchot, Lyotard, Levinas, Irigaray, Descombes and many others) do not stand in a 'tradition' or belong to a school, but rather 'each entertains a complex rapport' to 'the Husserlian, the Marxian, the Heideggerian, and the Nietzschean traditions' (p. 3). When Nancy writes of 'those who return, as though nothing had happened, to the humanist subject', clearly he has in mind Ferry and Renaut.

In an interview with Nancy, Derrida (1995a, p. 256) disputes Nancy's interpretation of the 'liquidation of the subject', and, discussing the discourse concerning 'the question of the subject' in France over the last twenty-five years, suggests instead the slogan, 'a return to the subject, the return of the subject'.[18] He begins the interview by briefly tracing the place of the subject in Lacan (the decentring of the subject), in Althusser (its interpellation), and in Foucault ('a history of subjectivity' and 'a return to a certain ethical subject').[19]

> For these three discourses (Lacan, Althusser, Foucault) and for some of the thinkers they privilege (Freud, Marx, Nietzsche), the subject can be re-interpreted, re-stored, re-inscribed, it certainly isn't 'liquidated'. The question 'who', notably in Nietzsche, strongly reinforces this point. This is also true of Heidegger, the principle reference or target of the *doxa* we are talking about. The ontological questioning that deals with the *subjectum*, in its Cartesian and post-Cartesian forms, is anything but a liquidation. (Derrida, 1995a, p. 257)

The attribution of the 'liquidation' of the subject to a Nietzschean poststructuralism—an attribution underlying the polemical attacks of Ferry and Renaut and also of a French kind of neo-liberalism—operates polemically to identify its target only by ignoring the time, place and logical space of the subject, its multiple genealogy within the history of modern philosophy and its active reinterpretation and reinscription. What this tells us is that the *problematique* of the subject, as it has developed in France over the last twenty-five years, cannot be reduced to homogeneity.

Derrida's response to Nancy in the interview is both complex and detailed, covering extensive territory and raising fresh sources for inquiry. While it may be true to say that Derrida's discussion focuses upon an explication of themes in Heidegger (and Levinas to a lesser degree) in relation to a certain *responsibility* and the question of the subject, he makes reference to the entire history of the metaphysics of subjectivity, mentioning along the way many of the most prominent thinkers in the last twenty-five years of French philosophy. I think it is useful to linger a while to consider Derrida's (1995a, p. 264) description of the way in which the central 'hegemony' of the subject was put into question again in the 1960s at a point when the question of time and of the other became linked to the interest in Husserl's discourse:

> It was in the 1950s and 1960s, at the moment when an interest in these difficulties [i.e. the dislocation of the absolute subject from the other and from time] developed in a very different way (Levinas, Tran-Duc-Thao, myself) and following moreover other trajectories (Marx, Nietzsche, Freud, Heidegger), that the centrality of the subject began to be displaced ... But if certain premises are found 'in' Husserl, I'm sure that one could make a similar demonstration in Descartes, Kant, and Hegel ... This would have at least the virtue of de-simplifying, of 'de-homogenizing' the reference to something like The Subject.

Derrida is turned to Heidegger by Nancy, and he refers to the act by which Heidegger substitutes a concept of *Dasein* for a concept of the subject simultaneously recalling 'the essential ontological fragility of the ethical, juridical, and political foundations of democracy' (p. 266) which 'remain essentially sealed within a philosophy of the subject' (p. 266). The question and task, Derrida suggests, is to develop an ethics, a politics and an 'other' democracy—he refers elsewhere to a 'democracy to come' based upon Nietzsche's understanding (see below)—that is, 'another type of responsibility' which would safeguard us against the 'worst' anti-democratic intrusions (i.e. National Socialism in all its forms). As Derrida (1995a, p. 272) puts it:

> In order to recast, if not rigorously re-found a discourse on the 'subject,' on that which will hold the place (or replace the place) of the subject (of law, of morality, of politics—so many categories caught up in the same turbulence), one has to go through the experience of deconstruction.[20]

Significantly, Derrida suggests that *Dasein*, in *Being and Time*, in spite of the questions it has raised and the spaces it has opened up for thinking, still occupies a place similar or analogous to that of the transcendental subject because it has been determined on the basis of a series of oppositions not sufficiently scrutinised. These oppositions include all the essential predicates of which subjects are the subject and which are ordered around being-present [*étant-présent*] such as 'presence to self ... identity to self, positionality, property, personality, ego, consciousness, will, intentionality, freedom, humanity, etc.' (p. 274). We shall not follow Derrida in any detailed way into his excursus on the 'yes, yes' or the affirmation, as he says, not addressed first to a subject but rather bids to a certain responsibility not reducible to and beyond the traditional category of the subject. Suffice to say here that

Derrida locates this responsibility in 'that to which one *cannot and should not* submit the other in general'; in the 'who' of friendship that provokes 'conscience' and therefore opens up responsibility (p. 275). This 'who' of friendship, he claims, belongs to the existential structure of *Dasein* and 'precedes every subjectal determination' (p. 275), referring to both Nancy's *Inoperative Community* and Blanchot's *The Unavowable Community*. He says clearly:

> The origin of the call that comes from nowhere, an origin in any case that is not yet a divine or human 'subject,' institutes a responsibility that is to be found at the root of all ulterior responsibilities (moral, juridical, political), and of every categorical imperative. (Derrida, 1995a, p. 276)

This figure of responsibility can be approached also through Levinas's understanding of subjectivity of the *hostage* where 'the subject is responsible for the other before being responsible for himself as "me"' (p. 279).

While the discourses of Heidegger and Levinas disrupt a certain traditional humanism they remain 'profound humanisms *to the extent that they do not sacrifice sacrifice*' (p. 279). In other words, both thinkers tend to be humanists to the extent that only sacrifice of human life is forbidden, not life in general. Let me quote Derrida (1995a, pp. 281–282) yet again—a tortuous passage but one that rescues (finally) the significance of the title 'Eating Well' and casts light upon the remarks above.

> If the limit between the living and the nonliving now seems to be as unsure ... as that between 'man' and 'animal', and if ... the ethical frontier no longer rigorously passes between the 'Thou shalt not kill' (man, thy neighbour) and the 'Thou shalt not put to death the living in general' ... then, as concerns the 'Good' [*Bien*] of every morality, the question will come back to determining the best, most respectful, most graceful, and also the most giving way of relating to the other and of relating the other to the self. For everything that happens at the edge of the orifices (of orality, but also of the ear, the eye—and all the 'senses' in general) the metonymy of 'eating well' [*bien manger*] would always be the rule.[21]

The explication of 'who' in relation to sacrifice at once allows Derrida to emphasise the originality of Heidegger's and Levinas's discourses while recognising their humanisms, and the way they break from traditional humanism. (He suggests that Heidegger was a Judeo-Christian thinker.) At the same time it allows Derrida to foreshadow the notion of responsibility for an ethics, and politics, to come which springs from the relation to the other.[22] Certainly it is the case, against Ferry and Renaut and other anti-Nietzscheans, that Derrida does not do away with the subject. He does not 'eliminate' or 'liquidate' although he does deconstruct the sovereign subject and the history of the subject. For Derrida, as his comment almost thirty years ago should remind us—a comment I used to open this paper— the notion of the subject is something one cannot get along without. It is never a question of doing without it so much as 'knowing where it comes from and how it functions'.

In relation to the question of democracy, Derrida (1994a, pp. 41–42) resists the temptation to conclude that Nietzsche is an enemy of democracy in general and has nothing to offer in the name of 'a democracy to come'. His argument denies a simple-minded nihilism as it applies to the subject, to notions of political agency and to the Idea of democracy: 'Since, in my eyes, Nietzsche criticises a particular form of democracy in the name of "democracy to come", I don't consider Nietzsche to be an *enemy of democracy in general*.' Derrida suggests that this move is to open up the difference between a notion of democracy, 'which while having something in common with what we understand by democracy today ... is reducible neither to the contemporary reality of "democracy" nor to the ideal of democracy informing this reality or fact'. It is this difference that Derrida indicates he has explored at length in *Spectres de Marx* (1993). While, as Derrida maintains, one cannot subscribe to all of what Nietzsche has written concerning the democracy of his day, he identifies 'particular risks in what he foregrounded under the name of "democracy"' and 'There are at the same time critical and genealogical motifs in Nietzsche which *appeal to a democracy to come*' (Derrida, 1994a, pp. 41–42).[23]

Richard Beardsworth, observes that Derrida's work, in distinction to both Nietzsche and Heidegger, affirms both technology and democracy and he asks the following question:

> Although the promise of democracy is not the same as either the *fact* of democracy or the regulative *idea* (in the Kantian sense) of democracy, deconstruction does 'hear' *différance* more in a democratic organisation of government than in any other political model; and there are no new models to be invented. If I understand you correctly, your affirmation of democracy is, in this respect, a demand for the sophistication of democracy, such a refinement taking advantage, in turn, of the increasingly sophisticated effects of technology. (Derrida, 1994a, p. 18)

Beardsworth poses the question in relation to a number of pertinent observations: first, that 'democratic institutions are becoming more and more unrepresentative in our increasingly technicised world'; second, that 'the media are swallowing up the constitutional machinery of democratic institutions, furthering thereby the depoliticisation of society and the possibility of populist demagogy'; third, that 'resistance to this process of technicisation is at the same time leading to virulent forms of nationalism and demagogy in the former Soviet empire'; and, finally, 'the rights of man would seem an increasingly ineffective set of criteria to resist this process of technicisation (together with its possible fascistic effects) given this process's gradual effacement of the normative and metaphysical limit between the human and the inorganic' (p. 18).

Derrida responds by contemplating the nature of contemporary acceleration of technicisation and the relation between technical acceleration—a product of the so-called technosciences—and politico-economic processes, which relates rather to the structure of decision-making. In relation to these two kinds of acceleration, Derrida asks, 'what is the situation today of democracy?' His response is worthy of noting:

'Progress' in arms-technologies and media-technologies is incontestably causing the disappearance of the site on which the democratic used to be situated. The site of representation and the stability of the location which make up parliament or assembly, the territorialisation of power, the rooting of power to a particular place, if not to the ground as such—all this is over. The notion of politics dependent on this relation between power and space is over as well, although its end must be negotiated with. I am not just thinking here of the present forms of nationalism and fundamentalism. Technoscientific acceleration poses an absolute threat to Western-style democracy as well, following its radical undermining of locality. Since there can be no question of interrupting science of the technosciences, it's a matter of knowing how a democratic response can be made to what is happening. This response must not, for obvious reasons, try to maintain at all costs the life of a democratic model of government which is rapidly being made redundant. If technics now exceeds democratic forms of government, it's not only because assembly or parliament is being swallowed up by the media. This was already the case after the First World War. It was already being argued then that the media (then the radio) were forming public opinion so much that public deliberation and parliamentary discussion no longer determined the life of a democracy. And so, we need a historical perspective. What the acceleration of technicisation concerns today is the frontiers of the nation-state, the traffic of arms and drugs, everything that has to do with inter-nationality. It is these issues which need to be completely reconsidered, not in order to sound the death-knell of democracy, but in order to rethink democracy *from within these conditions*. (Derrida, 1994, pp. 57–58).

Derrida maintains that since technics have obliterated 'locality', the future of democracy must be thought in global terms. It is no longer possible to be a democrat 'at home' and wait to see what happens 'abroad'. In emphasising the call to a world democracy Derrida suggests the stakes of a 'democracy to come' can no longer be contained within frontiers or depend upon the decisions of a group of citizens or a nation, or group of nations. The call is for something new which is both more modest and yet also more ambitious than any overriding concept of the universal, the cosmopolitan or the human. Derrida distinguishes the difference between a rhetorical sense of democracy as politics that transcends borders (as one might speak of the United Nations) and what he calls a 'democracy to come'. The difference exhibits itself in decisions made in the name of the Rights of Man which, he suggests, 'are at the same time alibis for the continued inequality between singularities'. He indicates that we need to invent new concepts—concepts other than that of 'state', 'superstate', 'citizen' and so forth for what he has called the new International (Derrida, 1993). He says:

The democracy to come obliges one to challenge instituted law in the name of an indefinitely unsatisfied justice, thereby revealing the injustice of calculating justice whether this be in the name of a particular form of democracy or of the concept of humanity. (Derrida, 1994a, pp. 60–61).

Elsewhere Derrida (1994b) explains what he means by deconstructing the foundations of international law. While international law is a good thing, it is nevertheless rooted in the Western concept of philosophy—as he says, 'in its mission, its axiom, in its languages'—and the Western concept of state and sovereignty, which acts as a limit. In order to rethink the international order and think of a 'democracy to come' we must deconstruct the foundations of international law and the international organisations built upon it. The second limit is that the international organisations are governed by a number of powerful, rich states, including the United States.

Derrida here is attempting 'to deconstruct the political tradition not in order to depoliticize but in order to interpret differently the concept of the political'.

> So justice and gift should go beyond calculation, which doesn't mean that we shouldn't calculate, we should calculate it as rigorously as possible but there is a point or a limit beyond which calculation must fail ... And so what I tried to think or to suggest is a concept of the political and of democracy which would be compatible, which could be articulated with these impossible notions of the gift and justice. (Derrida, 1994b)

It might be argued that the prospect of a critical pedagogy of difference, of a genuinely multicultural and internationalist pedagogy suitable for the future, is located at the interstices and in the interplay between a 'democracy to come' and a 'subject to come', a global subject whose critical function it is to both initiate and interrogate the new International.

Notes

1. Nietzsche, 1968, p. 270.
2. From the discussion following 'Structure, Sign and Play in the Discourses of the Human Sciences' (see Macksey & Donato, 1970, p. 271).
3. For a clear account of deconstruction and its American reception and mediation (especially at the hands of Paul de Man) as a school of literary criticism, see Rorty, 1995. Rorty provides an exemplary account of both deconstructionist theory and the two main lines of (analytic) criticism against Derridean philosophy. For a contextual account of deconstructionism within the French intellectual scene see Ffrench (1995), who suggests, following de Man, that the importation of linguistics into the discourse of literary criticism enabled the turn from aesthetics of the text to the modalities of its production (p. 17).
4. See my 'Poststructuralism and the Philosophy of the Subject', chapter 1, in Peters, 1996.
5. Judith Butler's (1987, p. 175) comment is entirely apposite here: 'The twentieth-century history of Hegelianism in France can be understood in terms of two constitutive moments: (1) the specification of the subject in terms of finitude, corporeal boundaries, and temporality and (2) the "splitting" (Lacan), "displacement" (Derrida), and eventual death (Foucault, Deleuze) of the hegelian subject'.
6. For an account on the importance of Nietzsche to poststructuralist thought and to Derrida, see Behler, 1991; Large, 1993; and Schrift, 1995, 1996; also see my 'Naming

the Multiple: Poststructuralism and Education' (Peters, 1998) and Trifonas, 1998, for an account of Derrida 'educational writings', especially his 'The Age of Hegel'.

7. 'The Question of Style' is the title of Derrida's presentation to the Nietzsche conference at Cerisy-la-Salle in 1972, which was later extended into *Spurs: Nietzsche's Styles* (1978a).

8. There have been a number of attempts to apply Derrida's ideas to pedagogy. Gregory Ulmer (1985) has outlined a project after-Derrida, especially in the areas of media and cultural studies, that he calls applied grammatology, where students are encouraged to experience theory directly in performance. See his home page at: <http://www.ucet.ufl.edu/~gulmer>. See also Vincent Leitch, 1996, especially chapters 'Teaching Deconstructively' and 'Postmodernism, Pedagogy and Cultural Criticism'.

9. This is Schrift's (1995, p. 24) construction. He writes, 'Derrida develops his deconstructive critique of the subject as a privileged center of discourse in the context of his project of delegitimizing authority, whether that authority emerges in the form of the author's domination of the text, or the tradition's reading of the history of philosophy' (p. 25). Derrida's deconstructive critique of authority—the authority both of the text and of the history of philosophy—has an obvious relevance to pedagogy as a critique of authority of educational institutions and those that assume positions of authority in its name.

10. His questioning of pedagogical forms of writing is, perhaps, clearest in 'The Time of the Thesis: Punctuations' (Derrida, 1983), the text of a presentation given at the opening of a thesis defence based on published works at the Sorbonne in 1980. There Derrida divides his work into four phases: 1957–62; 1963–67; 1968–74; and the years after 1974. He says he registered his thesis with the title of 'The Ideality of the Literary Object' in 1957, which was concerned with using techniques of transcendental phenomenology to elaborate a new theory of literature. During the second period he says that he was trying to work out a 'not wholly formalizable ensemble of rules for reading, interpretation and writing' (p. 40). During each period, he relates his own activities to the form of the thesis and the structure of the *universitas* which, he says, 'has an essential tie with the ontological and logocentric onto-encyclopedic system' (p. 43). Later he states: deconstruction 'was not primarily a matter of philosophical contents, themes or theses, philosophemes, poems, theologemes or ideologemes, but especially and inseparably meaningful frames, institutional structures, pedagogical or rhetorical norms, the possibilities of law, of authority, of evaluation, and of representation in terms of its very market' (pp. 44–45).

11. See, for example, their reference, in the Preface to the English translation, to Victor Farias (p. xv). They also later became embroiled in the so-called Heidegger affair when Farias' book sparked a debate in the 1980s concerning alleged new revelations of Heidegger's Nazi involvement. See Ferry & Renaut's (1990b) *Heidegger and Modernity*.

12. Lilla (1994, p. 32, n. 38) makes the following useful remark:

> Ferry and Renaut have made two, not always compatible appeals to previous philosophies of the subject. One is to Kant, and specifically to the *Critique of Judgment*, wishing to avoid the transcendental presuppositions of the First Critique and the rigors of the Second, they have followed the increasingly common strategy of seeking in the Third an 'aesthetic' model for reflection on morals and politics ... A second appeal is to Fichte, specifically to his earliest work: here they discover a 'non-metaphysical' philosophy of the subject that makes room for intersubjective experience and permits a critical analysis of history.

The first appeal might be considered curious in the light of the fact that Lyotard first moved in this direction in the early 1980s to sustain his notion of heterogenous language games. See his essay 'Answering the Question; What is Postmodernism?', an appendix to *The Postmodern Condition* (1984).

13. For the full text of the letter and Derrida's response, originally published in the *Cambridge Review* in 1992, see Derrida's (1992) '*Honoris Causa*: "This is *also* extremely funny"'. For a recent and balanced account of the affair, see Joseph Margolis, 1994.

14. For a full discussion of this matter, see 'Monoculturalism, Multiculturalism and Democracy: The politics of difference or recognition?', chapter 10, in Peters, 1996.

15. See, for example, Derrida's (1976, p. 19) comment: 'Radicalizing the concepts of *interpretation, perspective, evaluation, difference*, and all the "empiricist" or nonphilosophical motifs that have constantly tormented philosophy throughout the history of the West, and besides, have had nothing but the inevitable weakness of being produced in the field of philosophy, Nietzsche, far from remaining simply (with Hegel and as Heidegger wished) within metaphysics, contributed a great deal to the liberation of the signifier from its dependence or derivation with respect to the logos and the related concept of truth or the primary signified, in whatever sense that is understood.' Derrida begins the 'Exergue' to his *Of Grammatology* by focusing our attention on the ethnocentrism which has controlled our notion of writing and addresses the notion further in Part II, *Nature, Culture, Writing*. This would be an appropriate starting point for Gutmann if she was interested in 'deconstructionism' in relation to the question of ethnocentrism. Still the best short commentary, in my view, on Derrida in relation to Nietzsche, Heidegger, Freud, is Gayatri Chakravorty Spivak's (1976) Translator's Preface to *Of Grammatology*.

16. Of all the essays, perhaps the most interesting and most relevant for my puposes here is Philippe Raynaud's (1997) 'Nietzsche as Educator'. Raynaud wants to approach Nietzsche's oeuvre directly rather than through his 'French admirers' to ask about the kind of philosophy possible today, Nietzsche's relation to the Enlightenment and his critique of modern ideals. His interpretation is, I think, insightful: 'The task for democratic political thinking is analogous to that which I have tried to define for philosophy: as an antidote to the modern spirit, Nietzsche's thought should be taken by modernity as a privileged means for self-criticism. It is in that respect, more than as a master of truth, that Nietzsche is an *educator*.'

17. This section is based upon an expansion and reconsideration of a couple of points I first advanced in 'Introduction: Naming the multiple' (Peters, 1998).

18. The interview with Jean-Luc Nancy entitled ' "Eating Well," or The Calculation of the Subject' was originally published in *Cahiers Confrontation*, 20 (Winter 1989), an issue called 'Après le sujet qui vient' (After the Subject Who Comes). All references in this chapter are to the full interview now published in *Points ... Interviews, 1974–1994* (Derrida, 1995a). A note (Derrida, 1995c, p. 473) recording the circumstances and bibliographic history surrounding the interview, used to first present the interview in *Cahiers*, is repeated in *Points*. I think it is worth repeating here: 'Jacques Derrida was unable to write a text in time for *Topoi* (the journal in which this interview was initially published in English translation in October 1988 [vol. 7, no. 2]; the issue has since been re-edited as a book: *Who Comes After the Subject?* Ed. Eduardo Cadava, Peter Connor and Jean-Luc Nancy [New York: Routledge, 1991]. He proposed that we do an interview instead. The latter, however, took place too late to be integrally transcribed and translated in *Topoi*, which was able to publish only about half of it. It appears here almost in its entirety (although not without the omission of certain developments whose themes were announced in *Topoi*: the whole would have been both too long and occasionally too far afield from the main theme).'

19. Derrida (1995a, p. 256) notes 'As for Foucault's discourse, there would be different things to say according to the stages of its development'. This remark is important for it reveals the complexity of the question of the subject in the thought of *one* thinker which demonstrates the inadequacy of the generalised description the 'liquidation' of the subject as it applies to the whole of post-war French philosophy. On the 'stages' of the history of subjectivity in the discourses of Heidegger and Foucault (and the parallels between them), see Dreyfus (1996, 1998). Dreyfus (1998, p. 1), in particular, demonstrates, I think, the inadequacy of the notion that the subject has been 'liquidated' in either Heidegger or Foucault. He writes: 'Whatever their similarities and

differences, one thing that Heidegger and Foucault clearly have in common is that they are both critical of the Cartesian idea of a self-transparent subject and the related Kantian ideal of autonomous agency. Yet neither denies the importance of human freedom. In Heidegger's early work the subject is interpreted as *Dasein*—a non-autonomous-thrown way of being, yet who can change the field of possibilities in which it acts. In middle Heidegger, thinkers alone have the power to disclose a new world, while in later Heidegger, anyone is free to step back from the current world, enter one of a plurality of worlds and facilitate a change in the practices of one's society. For early Foucault the subject is reduced to a function of discourse; for middle Foucault writing can open up new worlds, and in later Foucault, freedom is understood as the power to question what is currently taken for granted, plus the capacity to change oneself. In short, while both Heidegger and Foucault reject the Enlightenment idea as an autonomous subject, they have a robust notion of freedom and action.' Dreyfus's observation expressed in his last sentence is important for pedagogy and educational theory for, following Heidegger and Foucault, it suggests that it is possible to posit a notion of the subject which is not autonomous in the traditional Cartesian–Kantian sense, yet nevertheless free and capable of action. What would a pedagogy-based such subject look like?

20. Invoking a certain notion of *responsibility* which is excessive in that it 'regulates itself neither on the principles of reason nor on any sort of accountancy', Derrida (1995a, p. 272) suggests that the subject is also 'a principle of calculability'—hence part of the title of the interview 'The Calculation of the Subject'. As he suggests, 'the subject is also a principle of calculability—for the political (and even, indeed, for the current concept of democracy, which is less clear, less homogenous, and less of a given than we believe or claim to believe, and which no doubt needs to be rethought, radicalized, and considered as a thing of the future), in the question of legal rights (including human rights, about which I would repeat what I have just said about democracy) and in morality' (Derrida, 1995a, p. 272). Yet, for us to arrive at a notion of responsibility that might carry with it the new possibilities and new meanings for the political and the moral, the calculation of the subject must pass through deconstruction.

21. The translator's note (n. 15, p. 475) says: 'The phrase in play here, "Il faut bien manger" (which is also the original title of the interview), can be read in at least two ways: "one must eat well" or "everyone has to eat". In addition, when the adverb "bien" is nominalized as "le Bien", there results the sense of "eating the Good". It is this multivalent sense that Derrida explores in the succeeding sentences'. I shall not attempt to précis Derrida's stunning and surprising 'turns' but will simply leave it as an enticement.

22. I think it is useful to refer to the way in which Derrida recognises how the question of the subject and of the living 'who', as he says, is at the heart of the most pressing concerns of modern societies. I shall summarise: decisions over birth and death, involving the treatment of sperm or ovum, surrogacy, genetic engineering, bio-ethics, bio-politics, euthanasia, organ removal and transplant.

23. Compared with Hollingdale's (1968, p. 89) remark: '*Democracy*: Nietzsche is known to be anti-democratic and is thought in this to be perversely opposing the whole general movement of the modern world. No need to agree or disagree here either: when Nietzsche was criticized for his moral theories he replied by asking "whether we have in fact become more moral", and we might likewise ask ourselves whether we have in fact become more democratic and whether in fact we want to. Do you consider every man and woman your equal, in every respect, in any respect? What does political democracy *mean*? Is it separable from industrial democracy? Who really *rules* (do you rule?). Are we any closer now to *cultural* democracy, to an actual equivalence of capacity between man and man, than we were in 1888 when *Twilight of the Idols* and *The Anti-Christ* were written?'

References

Behler, E. (1991) *Confrontations: Derrida, Heidegger, Nietzsche*, trans. S. Taubeneck (Stanford, Stanford University Press).

Butler, J. (1987) *Subjects of Desire: Hegelian reflections in twentieth-century France* (New York, Columbia University Press).

Cadava, E., Connor, P. & Nancy, J.-L. (eds) (1991) *Who Comes After the Subject?* (New York, Routledge).

Derrida, J. (1976) *Of Gammatology*, trans. G. C. Spivak (Baltimore & London, Johns Hopkins University Press).

Derrida, J. (1978a) *Spurs: Nietzsche's Styles*, trans. B. Harlow (Chicago, Chicago University Press).

Derrida, J. (1978b) Structure, Sign and Play in the Discourse of the Human Sciences, in: *Writing and Difference*, trans. A. Bass (Chicago, University of Chicago Press), pp. 278–293.

Derrida, J. (1981) *Positions*, trans. A. Bass (Chicago, University of Chicago Press).

Derrida, J. (1982) The Ends of Man, in: *Margins of Philosophy*, trans. A. Bass (Chicago, University of Chicago Press), pp. 109–136.

Derrida, J. (1983) The Time of the Thesis: Punctuations, in: A. Montefiore (ed.), *Philosophy in France Today* (Cambridge, Cambridge University Press), pp. 34–50.

Derrida, J. (1985) Otobiographies: The teaching of Nietzsche and the politics of the proper name, trans. A. Ronell, in: C. V. McDonald (ed.), *The Ear of the Other: Otobiography, transference, translation*, trans. P. Kamuf (New York, Schocken Books), pp. 1–38.

Derrida, J. (1993) *Spectres de Marx* (Paris, Editions Galileé).

Derrida, J. (1994a) Nietzsche and the Machine: An interview with Jacques Derrida by Richard Beardsworth, *Journal of Nietzsche Studies*, 7, pp. 7–66.

Derrida, Jacques (1994b) Roundtable Discussion with Jacques Derrida, transcribed by J. Christian Guerrero, Villanova University, 3 October 1994, located at: <http://www.lake.de/home/lake/hydra/vill1.html>.

Derrida, Jacques (1995a) 'Eating Well', or the Calculation of the Subject, in: E. Weber (ed.), *Points ... Interviews, 1974–1994*, trans. P. Kamuf & others (Stanford, Stanford University Press), pp. 255–287.

Derrida, J. (1995b) *Honoris Causa*: 'This is *also* extremely funny', in: E. Weber (ed.), *Points ... Interviews, 1974–1994*, trans. P. Kamuf & others (Stanford, Stanford University Press), pp. 399–421.

Derrida, J. (1995c) Is There a Philosophical Language?, in: E. Weber (ed.), *Points ... Interviews, 1974–1994*, trans. P. Kamuf & others (Stanford, Stanford University Press).

Descombes, V. (1980) *Modern French Philosophy*, trans. L. Scott-Fox & J. Harding (Cambridge, Cambridge University Press).

Descombes, V. (1997) Nietzsche's French Moment, in: L. Ferry & A. Renaut (eds), *Why We Are Not Nietzscheans*, trans. R. de Loaiza (Chicago & London, University of Chicago Press), pp. 70–91.

Dreyfus, H. (1996) Being and Power: Heidegger and Foucault, *International Journal of Philosophical Studies*, 4 (1996).

Dreyfus, H. (1998) Heidegger and Foucault on the Subject, Agency and Practices, at: <http://ist-socrates.berkeley.edu/~hdreyfus/html/paper_heidandfoucault.html>.

Engel, P. (1994) The Decline and Fall of French Nietzschero-Structuralism, in: B. Smith, *European Philosophy and the American Academy* (La Salle, IL, Hegeler Institute), pp. 21–42.

Ferry, L. & Renaut, A. (1990a) *French Philosophy of the Sixties: An Essay on antihumanism*, trans. M. Cattani (Amherst, University of Massachusetts Press).

Ferry, L. & Renaut, A. (1990b) *Heidegger and Modernity*, trans. F. Philip (Chicago & London, University of Chicago Press).

Ferry, L. & Renaut, A. (1991) *Pourquoi nous ne sommes pas nietzschéens* (Paris, Éditions Grasset & Fasquelle).

Ferry, L. & Renaut, A. (1997) What Must First Be Proved Is Worth Little, in: L. Ferry & A. Renaut (eds), *Why We Are Not Nietzscheans*, trans. R. de Loaiza (Chicago & London, University of Chicago Press), pp. 92–109.

Ferry, L. & Renaut, A. (eds) (1997) *Why We Are Not Nietzscheans*, trans. R. de Loaiza (Chicago & London, University of Chicago Press).

Ffrench, P. (1995) *The Time of Theory: A history of Tel Quel 1960–1983* (Oxford, Clarendon Press).

Gutmann, A. (1994) Introduction, *Multiculturalism: Examining the politics of recognition*, ed. and introduced by Amy Gutmann (Princeton, NJ, Princeton University Press).

Hollingdale, R. J. (1968) Introduction to F. Nietzsche, *Twilight of the Idols* and *The Anti-Christ*, trans. R. J. Hollingdale (Harmondsworth, Penguin).

Large, Duncan (1993) Translator's Introduction to S. Kofman, *Nietzsche and Metaphor* (London, Athlone Press), pp. vii–xl.

Leitch, V. (1996) *Local Effects, Glocal Flows* (New York, State University of New York Press).

Lévy-Strauss, C. (1958) *Anthropologie structurale*, 2 vols (Paris, Plon).

Lilla, M. (ed.) (1994) *New French Thought: Political philosophy* (Princeton, NJ, & Chichester, UK, Princeton University Press).

Lyotard, J.-F. (1984) *The Postmodern Condition: A report on knowledge*, trans. G. Bennington & B. Massumi (Manchester, Manchester University Press).

Macksey, R. & Donato, E. (eds) (1970) *The Structuralist Controversy: The Languages of Criticism and the Sciences of Man* (Baltimore & London, Johns Hopkins University Press).

Margolis, J. (1994) Deferring to Derrida's Difference, in: B. Smith (ed.), *European Philosophy and the American Academy* (La Salle, IL, Hegeler Institute, Moinst Library of Philosophy), pp. 195–226.

Nancy, J.-L. (1991) Introduction, in: E. Cadava, P. O'Connor & J.-L. Nancy (eds), *Who Comes After the Subject?* (London & New York, Routledge), pp. 1–8.

Nietzsche, F. (1968) Principles of a New Evaluation, no. 490, Book 3, in: W. Kaufmann (ed.), *The Will to Power*, trans. W. Kaufmann & R. J. Hollingdale (New York, Vintage Books).

Peters, M. (1996) *Poststructuralism, Politics and Education* (Westport, CT, & London, Bergin & Garvey).

Peters, M. (1998) Introduction: Naming the Multiple, in: M. Peters (ed.), *Naming the Multiple: Poststructralism and education* (Westport, CT & London, Bergin & Garvey).

Raynaud, P. (1997) Nietzsche as Educator, in: L. Ferry & A. Renaut (eds), *Why We Are Not Nietzscheans*, trans. R. de Loaiza (Chicago & London, University of Chicago Press), pp. 141–157.

Rorty, R. Deconstruction, in: R. Selden (ed.), *The Cambridge History of Literary Criticism*, vol. 8, *From Formalism to Poststructralism* (Cambridge, Cambridge University Press).

Schrift, A. (1995) *Nietzsche's French Legacy: A genealogy of poststructuralism* (New York & London, Routledge).

Schrift, A. (1996) Nietzsche's French Legacy, in: B. Magnus & K. Higgins (eds), *The Cambridge Companion to Nietzsche* (Cambridge, Cambridge University Press), pp. 323–355.

Smith, B. (ed.) (1994) *European Philosophy and the American Academy*, (La Salle, IL, Hegeler Institute).

Spivak, G. C. (1976) Translator's Preface, in: J. Derrida, *Of Grammatology* (Baltimore & London, Johns Hopkins University Press).

Taylor, C. (1994) The Politics of Recognition, in: *Multiculturalism: Examining the politics of recognition*, ed. and introduced by Amy Gutmann (Princeton, NJ, Princeton University Press).

Trifonas, P. (1998) Jacques Derrida: The ends of pedagogy—from the dialectic of memory to the deconstruction of the institution, in: M. Peters (ed.), *Naming the Multiple: Poststructuralism and Education* (Westport, CT, & London, Bergin & Garvey).

Ulmer, Gregory (1985) *Applied Grammatology: Post(e)-Pedagogy from Jacques Derrida to Joseph Beuys* (Baltimore, Johns Hopkins University Press).

Willard, D. (1994) The Unhinging of the American Mind: Derrida as pretext, in: B. Smith, *European Philosophy and the American Academy* (La Salle, IL, Hegeler Institute), pp. 3–20.

7

Signal Event Context: Trace technologies of the habit@online

ROBERT LUKE
University of Toronto

Introduction: Web portals and personalised information space

Web portals—those online environments that encourage users to trade personal information for the opportunity to personalise the information space—are experiencing a considerable resurgence in popularity. Web portals are web sites that allow users to log on with a username and password and create their very own datastructure. This datastructure will then be reconstructed and presented to them according to the preferences registered in their 'user profile'. Portals are sites that cater to individual desire; they present the user with the opportunity not only to access the world online, but to design and control the flow of information within a personalised space. This sense of empowerment is founded on an economic imperative operating within 'push' technology—network processes that push select information to users once preferences have been registered in a user profile.

Portals commodify information and track users as they view various datasets within the online networks of World Wide Web and Wireless World Wide Web (W3 and W4) environments. User profiles and the habits and patterns of browsing behaviour are then tracked and used to assemble consumer demographic data. These data comprise the home online—a habitat, or 'habit@online'. The habit@ is in turn used to construct larger profiles and patterns of consumption which are then sold back to the user. Within the fluid architecture of online environments, 'There is no fixed self, only the habit of looking for one' (Wise, 2000, p. 303). This habit of looking is our habit@online: the patterns of our browsing behaviour reconstituted as a demographic representation of how we will engage and actualise ourselves as desiring-machines within the space of flows of networked capital (cf. Deleuze & Guattari, 1983). Users are encouraged to think of web portals as their online home, a customised and personalised habit@ that pushes welcome information to the user, based on the traced habits of past consumption of information-as-commodity.

Deconstruction of the discursive construction of online identity formation is vital. Derridean deconstruction offers us a grammar for understanding the identity formation of W3 and W4 environments from a position within the technology itself. By interrogating the location of online discourse with respect to the language or grammar of online identity formation, we can learn to escape from a technological determinism that seeks to construct a digital citizen solely under the rubric of consumption. We can learn how to (re)invest network processes for an empower-ment outside an economic imperative. While it is important to acknowledge that web portals and other technologies of online identity formation are not all bad, it is important to 'locate accountability' within technological systems (cf. Suchman, 2002). The social analysis of technology leads to finding ways of responding to and actively shaping the ways in which technology mediates our lives. By examining the 'grammars of action' (Agre, 1994) that induce users to act within prescribed network processes, we can better fashion interventions that take into account the affective investment induced by the technologies that suffuse daily life. '*The description of the relation between technology and language thus becomes crucial to any analysis of the social*' (Wise, 1997, p. 62), and this leads us into the sociotechnical construction of the habit@online, and the particular form of digital citizenship that proliferates in this electronic environment.

Context: The living archive of the habit@

The habit@online is the construction of the patterns of browsing behaviour. It encompasses the enculturation processes (and marketing processes) that entice people to personalise informational spaces within web portals, as well as the tracking of movements through these informational spaces. 'The habit@online is the digital *habitus*: the ways in which people are encouraged to use technology, based on informal learning structures and the formation of habits associated with technology use' (Luke, 2002). This habit@ is thus comprised of 'the structures characterizing a determinate class of conditions of existence [that] produce the structures of the *habitus*, which in their turn are the basis of the perception and appreciation of all subsequent experiences' (Bourdieu, 1990, p. 54). The 'determinate class of conditions' is the structure of the portal logic that reterrit-orialises the formation of online identity under the rubric of consuming information-as-commodity. The process of consumption is then itself consumed, as the habits of data surfing are tracked and used to produce elaborate consumer demographic profiles based on browsing habits. These are then sold back to the consumer in the form of push advertising. This push is the (re)presentation of past habits of consumption (of information-as-commodity) to the web user. Thus the habit@, like 'The *habitus*, a product of history, produces individual and collective practices—more history—in accordance with the schemes generated by history' (Bourdieu, 1990, p. 54). In the habit@, this is the browsing history, identified by the use of cookies that are stored on a user's hard drive. The ongoing creation of *habitus*, as enacted within the habit@online, thus 'ensures the active presence of past experi-ences' via a 'system of dispositions—a present past that tends to perpetuate itself into the future by reactivation in similarly structured practices' (Bourdieu, 1990, p. 54) into an active presence articulated from past browsing habits. These pro-cesses create cycles that 'generate dispositions objectively compatible with these conditions and in a sense pre-adapted to their demands' (Bourdieu, 1990, p. 54), precisely because these dispositions or data representations are based on past demands for information-as-commodity. As we shall see, 'the active presence of past experiences' aptly defines the discursive construction of identity with the habit@online.

The habit@online is a living archive operating with the trace technologies of user pattern and demographic (re)construction. Trace technologies are the surreptitious programs that follow users' movements through the datastructure: browser cookies, complex javascripts, java and database entities that tag and record a user's electronic footprints, or dataprints. The data collection of the habit@ is 'the act of *con*signing through *gathering together signs*. It is not only the traditional *consignatio*, that is, written proof, but what all *consignatio* begins by presupposing. *Consignation* aims to coordinate a single corpus, a system or a synchrony in which all the elements articulate the unity of an ideal configuration' (Derrida, 1995a, p. 3). The larger demographic profile of the Internet is a single corpus, broadly construed: the ideal configuration of capital flows within online networks. 'The archontic principle of the archive is also a principle of consignation, that is, of gathering together' (Derrida, 1995a, p. 3). That is to say, the person invested with the power of online capital creates the archive in [his] own image; the user, navigating through the habit@, is represented by the ways in which data preferences are stored within network environments. The 'gathering together' within an ideal configuration is the collection of demographic data which accrues to the individual identity constructed within online capital flows. The 'ideal configuration' is the logic of capital flows within the habit@online. The habit@ is

> Revolutionary and traditional [in the sense that it plays on the past modes
> of consumption and advertising even while it revolutionizes the space of
> flows of networked capital flows]. An *eco-nomic* archive in this double
> sense: it keeps, it puts in reserve, it saves, but in an unnatural fashion,
> that is to say in making the law (*nomos*) or in making people respect the
> law. … It has the force of law, of a law of the house (*oikos*), of the house
> as place, domicile, family, lineage, or institution. (Derrida, 1995a, p. 7)

In short, it is the demographic profile of your home in the habit@, labelling your place amongst the economy of commodity flows. The habit@ is punctuated by this 'archive fever' of data mining, to entice more consumption. As user habits are enculturated and encouraged, these habits become part of the flows of network capital.

As we are enticed to increase browsing and/or spending habits according to what is on the network, we are also influenced by (while we influence) the market. We become the market even as we track the market via W3 and W4 portals: 'the technical structure of the *archiving* archive also determines the structure of the *archivable* content in its very coming into existence and in its relationship to the future. The archivization produces as much as it records the event' (Derrida, 1995a, p. 17). The archive has a direct relationship to the future in so far as the past habits are re-presented for future consumption. That is, the habit@ is an archive wherein, while we watch stock quotes filter through our portals, we are tracked in this watching in a panoptic, pan*info*con that becomes the archive even as we create it, add to it, participate within it.

> In an enigmatic sense ... the question of the archive is not ... a question
> of the past. It is not the question of a concept dealing with the past that
> might *already* be at our disposal or not at our disposal, *an archivable
> concept of the archive*. It is a question of the future, the question of
> the future itself, the question of a response, of a promise and of a
> responsibility for tomorrow. The archive: if we want to know what that
> will have meant, we will only know in times to come. Perhaps. Not
> tomorrow but in times to come, later on or perhaps never. (Derrida,
> 1995a, p. 36)

We can know in the present what we were in the past, but this is a perpetual
present. This future tense is the perpetual present that articulates the archive
(habits) into present or pre-sent modes of production|consumption, enacting a
binary equation of recording habits: producing information-as-commodity that
is consumed by online users, which in turn is consumed by the trace technologies
of the digital habit@. We come into digital being without questioning this basic
premise of portal logic, accepting that we must sign up—and sign over—identity
to enter the habit@.

Event: The perpetual present of the habit@id:entity

Within the habit@ users construct a digital persona, a proxy that stands in for them
within online environments.[1] The construction of this online identity is an id:entity.
An entity is a piece of code that represents something else, that stands in for an
object or a programmable function. In the case of portal identity formation, the
user's id:entity is the representation of id, of desire and affect, as reformulated
within the habit@online. This habit@id:entity is always *in formation*; the user's
proxy is merely a codified representation of that user's habits as continually
collected and collated via the trace technologies of networked capital. 'In this sense
... the "unconscious" is no more a "thing" than it is any other thing, is no more
a thing than a virtual or masked consciousness' (Derrida, 1986a, p. 21); the
habit@id:entity is the user's online mask, a virtual proxy by which discourses of
desire and affect become part of the informational matrix of the corporate Internet.

The perpetual present and the data collection of the habit@ is 'a "past" that has
never been present, and which never will be, whose future to come will never be a
production or a reproduction in the form of presence' (Derrida, 1986a, p. 21). This
past has never been present because the moment it exists in the present (as such)
it becomes the past marker of the territory marked in the habit@. Its future to
come will never be a production or reproduction of presence because this presence
is in turn marked by the passing of signifiers (cookies, in this case) which are then
reconstituted as a demograph, in the past. Because presence/absence in the habit@
is only a simulacra, the aggregate past was never 'there' and the anticipated future
is merely one of passing again through data. This is the function of the trace
technologies of the habit@. The habit@id:entity is a centre of online discourse; it
mediates a presence that is 'not a fixed locus but a function, a sort of nonlocus in

which an infinite number of sign-substitutions [come] into play' (Derrida, 1978c, p. 280). The fluid nature of the habit@id:entity is a functional representation of online market proxies in constant renegotiation and informational articulation. It is an additive function in which our presence is deferred insofar as we are always mediated and represented by our id:entity, which stands in for our sense of self within online environments. We are never really 'there' because our id:entity is a function, not a fixed locus, that marks the way we differentiate ourselves and our identity.

The issue of data collection and demographic profiling is one of context: the habit@id:entity can be used in any given context, and this personal profile can be used to generate other contexts within the logic of digital capital flows. That is, every signifier or data demograph 'can break with every given context, and engender infinitely new contexts in an absolutely nonsaturable fashion. This does not suppose that the mark ["sign"] is valid outside its context [the site of its original production], but on the contrary that there are only contexts without any center of absolute anchoring' (Derrida, 1986b, p. 320). Within the habit@, this centre is the fluid location of the *function* of data collection and collation within which contexts are generated in order to sell more commodities. The id:entity itself is the centre of the habit@, in so far as it represents the form and function of data production and consumption within the space of flows of networked capital. Cookies and data demographics themselves have no 'absolute anchoring', no centre; they are independent of the networks that produce them. They are instead free-floating signifiers of commodity consumption (and so production because they produce the trail of consumption as the grounds for more consumption). They are reused to continually update profiles within an *ex stasis* (because they 'stand outside' id:entity formation while still inextricably linked) cycle of duplication, and perhaps even duplicity (Gandy, 1995).

The id:entity is the 'metonymy of the sign' (Spivak, 1976, p. xxiv), a supplement within the habit@ that acts as the mediated representative of the user, accumulating 'facts' about this user that are then shared and articulated within an ever-growing matrix continuum of information retrieval. 'The supplement adds itself, is a surplus, a plenitude enriching another plenitude, the *fullest measure* of presence. It cumulates and accumulates presence' (Derrida, 1976, p. 144). The user's presence online is the id:entity that stands as proxy for the user within the compiling of demographic profiles and habit-tracking collation. The accumulated presence is comprised of the history of browsing habits. This digital individual is 'vectoral' in Wark's terms (Wark, 1994), a 'technological assemblage' (Wise, 1998) that is itself a plenitude enriching another: always collated with the larger demograph of the habit@online. 'But the supplement supplements. It adds only to replace. It intervenes or insinuates itself *in-the-place-of*; if it fills, it is as if one fills a void. If it represents and makes an image, it is by the anterior default of a presence' (Derrida, 1976, p. 145) precisely because this 'anterior default of a presence' is literally that which comes before in the datamine of the habit@. The supplement is the id:entity, the proxy through which an image of the user is assembled, and according to which the demographic profile is written. Derrida continues:

> Compensatory [*suppléant*] and vicarious, the supplement is an adjunct, a subaltern instance which *takes-(the)-place* [*tient-lieu*]. As substitute, it is not simply added to the positivity of presence, it produces no relief, its place is assigned in the structure by the mark of an emptiness. Somewhere, something can be filled up *of itself*, can accomplish itself, only by allowing itself to be filled through sign and proxy. The sign is always the supplement of the thing itself. (Derrida, 1976, p. 145)

This thing is the user's id:entity; the sign is the demographic profile, the demograph, literally, that which is 'people written'. Just as 'people are imagined and encouraged to view themselves as sovereign, discreet economic units' (Cox, 2001) within demographic re-presentations of their online browsing habits, the supplement is, quite properly, a 'proximate' representation of the self within data flows. It stands in only as it is germane to consumption habits.

The supplement to data flows and habits is the accretion of habits and commodities that fill the lack—the need to consume information as commodity, to be *in formation*. The habit@id:entity is marked by

> the movement of *supplementarity*. One cannot determine the center and exhaust totalization because the sign which replaces the center, which supplements it, taking the center's place in its absence—this sign is added, occurs as a surplus, as a *supplement*. The movement of signification adds something, which results in the fact that there is always more, but this addition is a floating one because it comes to perform a vicarious function, to supplement a lack on the part of the signified. (Derrida, 1978c, p. 289)

The signified is the user for which the id:entity is a stand-in. The movement of supplementarity is the additive function of the habit@id:entity, which is in fact a vicarious function of constructing identity online. The history of browsing habits is constantly overwritten in an additive function of living amongst dataflows. The re-presentation of the past habits of browsing history anticipates a future according to this accretive process: 'With its ceaseless re-launchings, its failures, its superimpositions, its overwritings and reprintings, this history wipes itself out in advance since it programs itself, reproduces itself, and reflects itself by anticipation' (Derrida, 1995b, p. 99). This constant erasure is palimpsestic, defining the habit@id:entity as a ceaseless function of browsing patterns and history, habits, etc., endlessly repeated, superimposed as the id:entity is constantly updated and renewed. The id:entity is marked by a supplementarity that represents presence and identity in the habit@online: 'Representation regularly *supplements* presence. But this operation of supplementation ... is not exhibited as a break in presence, but rather as a reparation and a continuous, homogenous modification of presence in representation' (Derrida, 1986b, p. 313). The representation here is the code that stands in for the person online. It is modified according to the present habits of usage data, and articulated within the supplemental trace of a continuous and additive function of identity *in formation*.

The data collection infrastructure exists to predict consumer behaviour, perhaps, but more to the point it exists to monitor this behaviour, and to modify it according to past habits of consumption (consuming information-as-commodity) in order to produce more consumption. This collation does not preclude the collection of new and further habits, however, and in fact actively encourages similar consumer commodities and habits based on established patterns, premises, and preferences. The id:entity context is a fluid and open-ended information architecture, 'For a context to be inexhaustively determinable ... it at least would be necessary for the conscious intention to be totally present and actually transparent for itself and others, since it is a determining focal point of the context' (Derrida, 1986b, p. 327). The habit@id:entity is not absolutely determinable for the simple reason that it is a function of the network processes that are always open and chaotic. The id:entity is infinitely adaptable and adaptive to the habit@, always present in the structure of online signification.

The trace of the habit@ is the focal point of the context in the habit@online. The process of id:entity formation is not necessarily transparent to those who are subject to and of this trace, as not all users are aware of the extent to which their data is tracked, collected, collated, and sold back at them (and to other advertisers) in an effort to create the space of flows of network capital. If the 'conscious intention' of the habit@id:entity is the structure of the id:entity itself, and if there is no real transparency in the sense that the user is not aware of this data collection, then the context can never be absolutely determinable, since there could be any number of permutations of data generated by browsing habits. Once an intelligent agent[2] attached to the collection of data 'learns' what kinds of things a user likes and/or wants, it can and will suggest similar products in an attempt to lure the user into further engagement with the commodity flows online.[3]

Signal: Trace, technology, and the self *in formation*

The id:entity is a signifying agent, the digital signal, or signature, traced in the habit@. 'To write is to produce a mark that will constitute a kind of machine that is in turn productive, that my future disappearance in principle will not prevent from functioning and from yielding, and yielding itself to, reading and writing' (Derrida, 1986b, p. 316). The mark that is written is the trace of the habit@, the id:entity that is productive because this mark produces the demograph that in turn leads to the disappearance of presence into commodity flows and consumption processes in general. Derrida's concept of writing mirrors the habit@id:entity, the effect of living online, as there is a kind of writing present, where the trace of the habit@id:entity is recorded within demographic data that continues to exist as a commodity (and indeed is sold as such) well after the collection of this data.

> For the written to be written, it must continue to 'act' and to be legible even if what is called the author of the writing no longer answers for what he has written, for what he seems to have signed, whether he is provisionally absent, or if he is dead, or if in general he does not support,

> with his absolutely current and present intention or attention, the
> plenitude of his meaning, of that very thing which seems to be written 'in
> his name.' (Derrida, 1986b, p. 316)

The habit@ trace continues to 'act' in so far as it continues to constitute part of
the market (and marked) accumulation of data. It continues to be a commodity for
future market consideration, used to sell more advertising, which in turn is used
to attract more viewers. The signal or cookie of the id:entity continues to transmit
because it constitutes a part of the market even though it may no longer be
attached to a particular user. This trace conforms to Derrida's concept of writing,
for 'A written sign, in the usual sense of the word, is therefore a mark which
remains, which is not exhausted in the present of its inscription, and which can
give rise to an iteration both in the absence of and beyond the presence of the
empirically determined subject who in a given context, has emitted or produced
it' (Derrida, 1986b, p. 317). The habit@id:entity, the trace of the user in cyber-
space, remains to signal the past event of the user moving through a given
datascape. This track remains in the host company's databases, and even remains
on the user's hard drive in the form of a cookie until the user deletes the cookie,
or it expires (usually after several years).

But the concept of the written event is problematised, especially within online
environments, as 'a written sign carries with it a force of breaking with its context,
that is, the set of presences which organize the moment of its inscription. This force
of breaking is not an accidental predicate, but the very structure of the written'
(Derrida, 1986b, p. 317). Here too we see the same context of the signal within
online dataflows. For the force of breaking with the original context is the use of
data demographics to (re)constitute advertising revenue, to sell the commodity
according to how often it has been viewed (many sites count 'page hits', or visits; this
information is tracked within the database that records every movement within
a given datascape). Thus the moment that organises the inscription of the cookie
(both onto a user's computer and on the host database) becomes a separate context
from the reselling of this data back to the consumer (in the form of push advertising
meant to entice a user back to a given site) and to investors in the host company
as well. The user thus becomes a double mark(et) proxy: marked by the market and
simultaneously constitutive of this market. Derrida reminds us that

> one can always list a written syntagma from the interlocking chain in
> which it is caught or given [in the habit@, this is the cookie trail and
> database trace] without making it lose every possibility of functioning,
> if not every possibility of 'communicating' precisely. Eventually, one may
> recognize other such possibilities in it by inscribing or *grafting* it into
> other chains. No context can enclose it. Nor can any code, the code being
> here both the possibility and impossibility of writing, of its essential
> iterability (repetition/alterity). (Derrida, 1986b, p. 317)

These 'other possibilities' are achieved through the reselling of demographic data.
These data are taken out of their original context (their relationship to the user and

the specific pages viewed, for example), and used to sell the larger profile of the host site in general. The 'grafting' is the reuse and reconception of data footprints and cookies, recompiling data demographics and reusing data to sell and construct id:entity formation amongst commodity flows.

We can transpose Derrida's concept of différance to encompass that aspect of the supplement that we are using to describe the additive id:entity formation in the habit@. For within this habit@, the history of our browsing habits is collected and collated within ever-growing databases of accretive supplements that form our id:entity. The datamine refers to the present via trace, the tracking of user movements through data which then comprise the id:entity, the market proxy that pushes information and/as commodity flows at the user based on past consumption habits. These traces mark the territory of past habits.

> It is because of *différance* that the movement of signification is possible only if each so-called 'present' element, each element appearing on the scene of presence, is related to something other than itself, thereby keeping within itself the mark of the past element, and already letting itself be vitiated by the mark of its relation to the future element, this trace being related no less to what is called the future than to what is called the past, and constituting what is called the present by means of this very relation to what it is not: what it absolutely is not, not even a past or a future as a modified present. (Derrida, 1986a, p. 13)

The perpetual present within portals is 'the scene of presence', the tracking of the id:entity within dataflows 'Which (is) (simultaneously) spacing (and) temporization' (Derrida, 1986a, p. 13). It is the creation of an identity marker that is constantly deferred, accreted, discretely, within the subtle collection of data footprints.

The id:entity is vitiated, decayed; the mark of the past gives way to the present mark(er) of presence within the habit@online, and the mark of the present is always overwritten. This past mark is kept in reserve only in so far as it can relate to the present—the pre-sent (because based on past habits) future mark that overwrites the past mark even while building on it. 'For the economic character of *différance* in no way implies that the deferred presence can always be found again, that we have here only an investment that provisionally and calculatedly delays the perception of its profit or the profit of its perception' (Derrida, 1986a, p. 20). This deferred presence is consumed in the perpetual present, and 'In this context, and beneath this guise, the unconscious is not, as we know, a hidden, virtual, or potential self-presence. It differs from, and defers, itself; which doubtless means that it is woven of differences, and also that it sends out delegates, representatives, proxies; but without any chance that the giver of proxies might "exist," might be present, be "itself" somewhere, and with even less chance that it might become conscious' (Derrida, 1986a, pp. 20–21). These proxies are the id:entities that accrue online interest. They are collated into data demographs used by corporate data trackers to construct further datastructures to encourage consumption and production of more commodity flows.

The habit@id:entity is constituted by différance, a play on the multiple meanings of 'the verb *différer* [which] has two meanings which seem quite distinct' (Derrida, 1986a, p. 7)—'to defer and to differ' (Derrida, 1986a, p. 7, translator's note). To defer the id:entity is the supplementary and accretive nature of online data collation; to differ is represented within the personalised information portal, the perpetual present of additive identity formation that allows users to individualise a portal, even as the portal itself is paradoxically an assemblage of mass-produced information commodities. It is the way(s) in which these mass-market information-as-commodities are displayed within personalised portals that amounts to difference. But these instances of differing are based on the complex history of our browsing habits. Thus there is a rather complex re-turn of the self *in formation* (the informational self), even as the personal is articulated in the language of mass commodity construction.

The personal is slotted into a particular dataset according to the demograph. More and more powerful databases are able to grab datasets and point these to individual users to achieve the illusion of personalisation. This is the illusion of différance: '*Différer* in this sense is to temporize, to take recourse, consciously or unconsciously, in the temporal and temporizing mediation of a detour that suspends the accomplishment or fulfillment of "desire" or "will," and equally effects this suspension in a mode that annuls or tempers its own effect' (Derrida, 1986a, p. 8). Further, 'this temporization is also temporalization and spacing, the becoming-time of space and the becoming-space of time' (Derrida, 1986a, p. 8). To temporise is to delay, which is precisely what happens within id:entity formation: identity proper (as opposed to the proper(ty) identity) is constantly deferred, delayed, put on hold as more habits are amassed within the habit@online.

The trails of the habit@ constitute identity *in formation*, the informational structure of the id:entity. These data trails or tracks become identity, and in so doing erase the original impetus that constructed the initial formation. That is, there is a continual process of supplementarity in the constant and additive agglomeration of habits that constantly (re)constitute identity formation in an *ex stasis* cycle of endless (machinic) reproduction:

> Since the trace is not a presence but the simulacrum of a presence that dislocates itself, displaces itself, refers itself, it properly has no site— erasure belongs to its structure. And not only the erasure which must always be able to overtake it … but also the erasure which constitutes it from the outset as a trace, which situates it as the change of site, and makes it disappear in its appearance, makes it emerge from itself in its production. (Derrida, 1986a, p. 24)

This erasure does not really exist, but rather refers to identity formation as accretion —the production of id:entity. Within the différance of the habit@online, 'the present becomes the sign of the sign, the trace of the trace. It is no longer what every reference refers to in the last analysis. It becomes a function in a structure of generalized reference. It is a trace, and a trace of the erasure of the trace' (Derrida, 1986a, p. 24). This is the perpetual present of the habit@online. The sign of the habit@ is the id:entity of the user as tracked through the dataflows. This 'sign of the sign' is the habit@ identity formation as affect (desire) and effect (inventory), 'A past that has never been present' (Derrida, 1986a, p. 21), precisely because this present is always the past. As each data crumb is mined it is added to the database and becomes part of the larger structure of meaning (the profile of the id:entity). 'And the concept of trace, like that of *différance* thereby organizes, along the lines of these different traces and differences of traces ... the network which reassembles and traverses our "era" as the delimitation of the ontology of presence' (Derrida, 1986a, p. 21). Our signals are our movements in the habit@: 'we go through the detour of the sign. We take or give signs. We signal. The sign, in this sense, is deferred presence' (Derrida, 1986a, p. 9). Our relationship to technology is constituted within 'the detour of the sign' as our presence—our complete identity—is never complete but instead replete with supplementarity.

The signal event context of the habit@id:entity is the trace of the signal and its relation to the present and to the source, emitted within the present. This context is the data structure inhabited as the user navigates the informational matrices of the WWW.

> By definition, a written signature implies the actual or empirical nonpresence of the signer. But, it will be said, it also marks and retains his having-been present in a past now, which will remain a future now, and therefore in a now in general, in the transcendental form of nowness (*maintenance*). This general *maintenance* is somehow inscribed, stapled to present punctuality, always evident and always singular, in the form of a signature. This is the enigmatic originality of every paraph. For the attachment to the source to occur, the absolute singularity of an event of the signature and of a form of the signature must be retained: the pure reproducibility of a pure event. (Derrida, 1986b, p. 328)

The signature of the habit@ is the data trail of the id:entity in this nowness, and within a maintenance of a stable identity that enables the tracking to take place. That this id:entity is 'always evident and always singular' points to the personalisation of data flows within the portal logic. The signal of the id:entity is attached to the source or point of engagement with information within the commodified space of the network itself. The habit@id:entity formation is a continual process that never exists in any finite or complete form because it is always in formation, the self information within which 'The very idea of finitude is derived from the movement of this supplementarity' (Derrida, 1978b, p. 228). This continual supplementation is the additive structure of the network *function*.

To Conclude: The *khōra* or, Freud and the scene of surfing

The habit@online is a *khōra*, a place of id:entity formation. Derrida describes the discourse on the *khōra* as 'the opening of a place "in" which everything would, at the same time, come to take *place* and *be reflected*' (Derrida, 1995b, p. 104). Thus the habit@online, wherein id:entity formation is constructed *and* reflected, sold back at the user, is also a proxy or vessel for the user's identification. The *khōra* is a mirror within a mirror of identity formation and articulation, a '*mise en abyme* [that] affects the forms of discourse on *places*, notably political places, a politics of place entirely commanded by the consideration of sites [*lieux*] (jobs in the society, region, territory, country), as sites assigned to types or forms of discourse' (Derrida, 1995b, p. 104). Add to these sites the sites of web pages, the sites of id:entity construction among the space of flows of online, networked capital. The *khōra* is 'the place of inscription of *all that is marked on the world*' (Derrida, 1995b, p. 106), and is thus an apt descriptor for the habit@online, and especially the habit@id:entity formation. This place, as the habit@, refers to both the site—the location or point of data collection online—and to the activity of this collection, as 'everything that takes place in it'.

The habits that are collected within this *mise en abyme* constitute a narrative of identity formation (the id:entity). These habits can be said to be a narrative of online behaviour—in so far as they tell a tale of where the person has been within the datastructure—that forms a dizzying logic of p/re/packaged habit that is p/re/sold back on/to itself. 'Each tale is thus the *receptacle* of another. There is nothing but receptacles of narrative receptacles, or narrative receptacles of narrative receptacles. Let us not forget that receptacle, place of reception or harbouring/lodging (*hypodokhè*), is the most insistent determination ... of *khōra*' (Derrida, 1995b, p. 117). This is the logic of id:entity formation as constructed through the trace technologies of the habit@online. The *khōra* is a 'receptacle', an 'imprint-bearer' (Derrida, 1995b, p. 126), that leaves its imprint on sites visited, and it is this imprint (which is printed to the user's hard drive as well) that contains the demographic information. The habit@ itself thus becomes a receptacle for the imprints of the many and multiple id:entities that are tracked through the datasphere, which in turn are receptacles for our browsing habits.

The habit@online is representative of Freud's Mystic Writing Pad, producing the 'memory-traces' that constitute the trace technologies of the habit@: the retention, reception and repetition of an additive id:entity formation. Within the Mystic Writing Pad, 'memory-traces can only consist in permanent modifications of the elements of the systems' (Derrida, 1978b, p. 216), and it is these memory-traces that form the id:entity of the habit@. Like the Mystic Writing Pad, the habit@id:entity formation does in fact create 'a potential for indefinite preservation and an unlimited capacity for reception' (Derrida, 1978b, p. 222), in so far as this means the collection and collation of data demographics is a continual additive function of the network processes of trace technologies. Derrida recounts the concept of 'the memory-trace which, though no longer the neurological trace, is not yet "conscious memory" ... and of the *itinerant* work of the trace, producing and following its route, the trace which traces, the trace which breaks open its own path' which together 'produces the present past' (Derrida, 1978b, p. 214). This 'present past' is the presence of past habits pressed into present service via the articulation of the habit@id:entity and the trace of data demographics. The id:entity is a perpetual palimpsest, always written and inscribed with the present character(s) of browsing habits. The trace of movement(s) through the informational network produces an itinerant trail of points visited, pages browsed, information consumed. This trail, used to add to the user profile—the id:entity—of the web browser, is then used to produce more incentives or imperatives for further consumption, creating a discourse uroboros that begins where it ends, feeding off the materiality of its own economic tale.

A Supplement: Technology as pharmakon

The habit@id:entity is defined by the trace technologies of consumption and production. 'This trace is the erasure of selfhood, of one's own presence' (Derrida, 1978b, p. 230), precisely because the id:entity comes to stand in for the self. By so doing, the citizen self is negated in favour of a digital consumer. The digital consumer legitimises itself solely under the rubric of consumption, measuring participation as consumption, making this consumption the ground of media effect. Within web portals, the digital consumer can vote on a favourite restaurant, movie, nightclub, or bar, but this voting does not constitute a digital democracy. A digital democracy is not the menu-driven choice of a variety of objects to be consumed, but rather the opportunity and the ability meaningfully to examine, investigate and participate within the lived reality, including the datastructure (Sunstein, 2001b; 2001a).

The danger of constituting digital citizenship as consumption is that we then take over both the rhetoric and the space for the exercise of political agency. If the digital consumer model is the only conception of or avenue for digital participation, then we will live within a narrow and limited conception of a capitalist order. Centring the conception of digital participation around creating digital consumers instead of digital citizens means that 'The function of this center [is] not only to orient, balance, and organize the structure ... but above all to make sure that the organising principle of the structure [does] limit what we might call the *play* of the structure' since 'the center of the structure permits the play of its elements inside the total form' (Derrida, 1978c, p. 278). The menu driven database design of the space of flows of network capital confines the 'play' of the user in the network to that of commodity consumption. This is the field of possibility that 'excludes totalization. This field is in effect that of *play*, that is to say, a field of infinite substitutions only because it is finite, that is to say, because instead of being an inexhaustible field ... instead of being too large, there is something missing from it: a center which arrests and grounds the play of substitutions' (Derrida, 1978c, p. 289). This finite infinitude is the logic of the habit@ taken from a history of meaning (browsing habits) that is limited to the capital flows of and on the network. It is infinite because of the endless loops and permutations of data habits and the play within the id:entity formation.

We are in danger of consigning the rights to define digital citizenship to commercial interests when we let the law of the habit@ be established under an economic alary. Derrida states that

> electronic mail today, even more than the fax, is on the way to
> transforming the entire public and private space of humanity, and first

> of all the limit between the private, the secret (private or public), and the public or the phenomenal. It is only a technique, in the ordinary and limited sense of the term: at an unprecedented rhythm, in quasi-instantaneous fashion, this instrumental possibility of production, of printing, of conservation, and of destruction of the archive must inevitably be accompanied by juridical and thus political transformations. These affect nothing less than property rights, publishing and reproduction rights. (Derrida, 1995a, p. 17)

Thus we become property, constituted in and as data flows and formations within a *'metaphysics of the proper [le propre*—self-possession, propriety, property, cleanliness]' (Derrida, 1976, p. 26; see also Derrida, 1978a; 1986a, p. 3, translator's note 1). This *metaphysics of the proper* is the property relations defined by commodity consumption within the habit@. 'Derrida uses the word "metaphysics" very simply as shorthand for any science of presence' (Spivak, 1976, p. xxi), and the theory of the habit@ is a science of digital presence as the 'citizen' is discursively constructed as/in commodity flows of production and consumption within corporate conceptions of the public Internet.

If 'Technology ... is license to forget' (Winner, 1992; quoted in Wise, 1997), mirroring Plato's cautionary tale of Thoth and the origins of writing (Plato, 1995; see also Derrida, 1981), then the danger of the habit@online is that we will lose the ability to critically engage this important site of culture when the interface disappears into the *habitus* of technology use (cf. Wise, 1997). But 'Technology is a mode of revealing' (Heidegger, 1977, p. 319) as well, and retaining the ability to read the sites of digital culture is an important facet of reading the discursive construction of online identity formation. The WWW is a textual realm; it is also archival. It produces what Poster calls 'The mode of information [which] designates social relations mediated by electronic communication systems, which constitute new patterns of language' (Poster, 1989, p. 126). Deconstruction provides a grammar for understanding how online media construct knowledge and experience, as well as a path to a pedagogical praxis that focuses on the process of deconstructing these discursive constructions of reality as part of living in the mediated postmodern world (Poster, 1989). Contextual understanding of new technologies and their role in mediating knowledge is particularly important for understanding media effects (Goldman, 2000; Jay, 2000; Kincheloe & McLaren, 1994; Malpas, 2000). This is especially important for education that must account for the lived and material relations of the incipient digital era.

Like Derrida, Wise tells us that 'Our analysis [of technology] must resist totality and recognize that vision is partial' (Wise, 1997, p. 58).[4] That is, we can never achieve the position of the 'last metaphysician' but must always situate our analysis *in medias res*, within the continuum of media *in formation*. Wise posits 'a theory that recognizes objective material constraints as well as socially constructed constraints on the form and function of any technology' and argues 'that hegemony is carried through technological systems not only through the discourse deployed by and around that system or by symbolic capital articulated to it, but through affective investment and material asignifying practices, structures and constraints' (Wise, 1997, p. 58). By examining these practices, structures and constraints on the formation of online identity, we can escape from the economic imperative that will determine digital citizen as digital consumer. We can construct the habit@id:entity not solely under the rubric of production and consumption, but as a means to participate in the growing use of information and communication technologies within education, government, and daily life.

Notes

1. For an extensive discussion of the construction of a digital proxy in the habit@online, see Luke, 2002, which draws on Agre, 1994; Clarke, 1994.
2. Intelligent Agents (IAs) are software programs that push information and commodities at users based on stored and monitored preferences. IAs can have enormous benefits for various applications such as the Semantic Web (Berners-Lee, Hendler & Lassila, 2001). However, it is important that we retain the ability to interrogate the socio-technical nature of such technologies (Wise, 1998).
3. It should be noted that this kind of push advertising exists offline as well—direct mailings based on magazine subscriptions, shopping habits at your local supermarket are tracked and coupons and other consumer enticements are mailed to people who participate in frequent shopper programs and special member discount stores. The difference within online environments is the fact that these environments can now morph into a literal picture (in the way data is displayed) that is individual, with advertising featuring people from your demographic, enjoying the products you enjoy, maybe even looking like, and at, you.
4. See also Suchman, 2002; Lave & Wenger, 1991.

References

Agre, P. (1994) Surveillance and Capture: Two models of privacy, *Information Society*, 10, pp. 101–127.

Berners-Lee, T., Hendler, J., & Lassila, O. (2001) The Semantic Web, *Scientific American*, May.

Bourdieu, P. (1990) *The Logic of Practice* (orig. pub. 1980), trans. R. Nice (Stanford, CA, Stanford University Press).

Clarke, R. (1994) The Digital Persona and its Application to Data Surveillance *Information Society*, 10, pp. 77–92.

Cox, D. (2001, 1 February) Event-Scene 95: Site Unseen—Seeing, Mapping, Communicating, *Ctheory*, retrieved 5 June 2001 from <http://www.ctheory.net/text_file.asp?pick=228>.

Deleuze, G. & Guattari, F. (1983) *Anti-Oedipus: Capitalism and Schizophrenia* (orig. pub. 1972), trans. R. Hurley, M. Seem & H. Lane (Minneapolis, University of Minnesota Press).

Derrida, J. (1976) *Of Grammatology* (orig. pub. 1967), trans. G. C. Spivak (Baltimore & London, Johns Hopkins University Press).

Derrida, J. (1978a) La Parole Soufflée, trans. A. Bass, in: *Writing and Difference* (Chicago, University of Chicago Press), pp. 169–195.

Derrida, J. (1978b) Freud and the Scene of Writing, trans. A. Bass, in: *Writing and Difference* (Chicago, University of Chicago Press), pp. 196–231.

Derrida, J. (1978c) Structure, Sign and Play in the Discourse of the Human Sciences, trans. A. Bass, in: *Writing and Difference* (Chicago, University of Chicago Press), pp. 278–294.

Derrida, J. (1981) *Dissemination* (orig. pub. 1972), trans. B. Johnson (Chicago, University of Chicago Press).

Derrida, J. (1986a) Différance (orig. pub. 1972), trans. A. Bass, in: *Margins of Philosophy* (Chicago, University of Chicago Press), pp. 1–28.

Derrida, J. (1986b) Signature Event Context (orig. pub. 1972), trans. A. Bass, in: *Margins of Philosophy* (Chicago, University of Chicago Press), pp. 307–330.

Derrida, J. (1995a) *Archive Fever: A Freudian Impression* (orig. pub. 1995), trans. E. Prenowitz (Chicago, University of Chicago Press).

Derrida, J. (1995b) Khora (orig. pub. 1993), in: T. Dutoit (ed. & trans.), *On the Name* (Stanford, CA, Stanford University Press), pp. 89–131.

Gandy, O. H. J. (1995) It's Discrimination, Stupid!, in: I. A. Boal & J. Brook (eds), *Resisting The Virtual Life: The Culture and Politics of Information* (San Francisco, City Lights), pp. 35–48.

Goldman, A. (2000) Telerobotic Knowledge: A reliabilist approach, in: K. Goldberg (ed.), *The Robot in the Garden: Telerobotics and Telepistemology in the Age of the Internet* (Cambridge, MA, & London, MIT Press), pp. 126–142.

Heidegger, M. (1977) The Question Concerning Technology, in: D. F. Krell (ed.), *Martin Heidegger: Basic Writings from Being in Time (1927) to The Task of Thinking (1964)* (San Francisco, Harper San Francisco), pp. 311–341.

Jay, M. (2000) The Speed of Light and the Virtualization of Reality, in: K. Goldberg (ed.), *The Robot in the Garden: Telerobotics and Telepistemology in the Age of the Internet* (Cambridge, MA, & London, MIT Press), pp. 144–163.

Kincheloe, J. L. & McLaren, P. L. (1994) Rethinking Critical Theory and Qualitative Research, in: N. K. Denzin & Y. S. Lincoln (eds), *Handbook of Qualitative Research* (Thousand Oaks, London & New Delhi, Sage Publications), pp. 138–157.

Lave, J. & Wenger, E. (1991) *Situated Learning: Legitimate peripheral participation* (Cambridge, UK, & New York, Cambridge University Press).

Luke, R. (2002) Habit@online: Web portals as purchasing ideology, *Topia: A Canadian Journal of Cultural Studies*, 8, pp. 61–89.

Malpas, J. (2000) Acting at a Distance and Knowing from Afar: Agency and knowledge on the Internet, in: K. Goldberg (ed.), *The Robot in the Garden: Telerobotics and Telepistemology in the Age of the Internet* (Cambridge, MA, & London, MIT Press).

Plato (1995) *Phaedrus*, trans. A. Nehamas & P. Woodruff (Indianapolis & Cambridge, Hackett Publishing Company, Inc).

Poster, M. (1989) *Critical Theory and Poststructuralism* (Ithaca & London, Cornell University Press).

Spivak, G. C. (1976) Translator's Preface, in: *Of Grammatology* (Baltimore & London, Johns Hopkins University Press), pp. ix–lxxxvii.

Suchman, L. (2002) *Located Accountabilities in Technology Production*, retrieved 22 August 2002 from Department of Sociology, Lancaster University, <http://www.comp.lancs.ac.uk/sociology/soc039ls.html>.

Sunstein, C. (2001a) Democracy and the Internet, *Mots Pluriels*, 18, retrieved 30 August 2001 from <http://www.arts.uwa.edu.au/MotsPluriels/MP1801cs.html>.

Sunstein, C. (2001b) *Republic.com* (Princeton, NJ, Princeton University Press).

Wark, M. (1994) *Virtual Geography: Living with global media events* (Bloomington & Indianapolis, Indiana University Press).

Winner, L. (1992) *Autonomous Technology: Technics-out-of-Control as a Theme of Political Thought* (Cambridge, MA, & London, MIT Press).

Wise, J. M. (1997) *Exploring Technology and Social Space* (London & New Delhi, Sage Publications).

Wise, J. M. (1998) Intelligent Agency, *Cultural Studies*, 12:3, pp. 410–428.

Wise, J. M. (2000) Home: Territory and identity, *Cultural Studies*, 14:2, pp. 295–310.

8
Dewey, Derrida, and 'the Double Bind'

JIM GARRISON
Virginia Tech

> I recall that from the beginning the question of the trace was connected
> with a certain notion of labour, of doing and that what I called
> pragrammatology tried to link pragmatism and grammatology
>
> —Jacques Derrida[1]

The texts of Jacques Derrida seem inextricably connected to the word deconstruction, yet, Derrida insists, 'The word "deconstruction," like all other words,
acquires its value only from its inscription in a chain of possible substitutions ...
The word has interest only ... where it replaces and lets itself be determined
by such other words as ... "trace," "différance," "supplement"' (Kamuf, 1991,
p. 275). The reader immediately senses the elusiveness of Derrida's thought.
His writings do not limit themselves to merely making a point; they perform it.
His texts, by virtue of both their singularity and their intrinsic relation to generality,
perform the action of opening themselves to the incalculable, unpredictable, and
the non-programmatic. They exhibit his effort to call a response by the 'other' for
whose arrival they have opened the way. Always on the move, Derrida allows no
word, no concept, and no non-concept to master him or inhibit the play of
language. Derrida himself does not think deconstruction 'a good word' and
concludes, 'It deconstructs itself' (Kamuf, pp. 274, 275). Derrida lives in a
world without a stable center. Everyone does; that is one lesson his philosophy
teaches.

Explicating the texts of Derrida is exhausting enough; doing the same for
the often-misunderstood texts of Dewey multiplies the difficulty. Combining them
so as to reflect each critically in the mirror of the 'other' seems almost foolhardy;
like fools, I rush in. Substituting 'trace' for 'différance' the following passage
provides some excuse for my folly: 'We must begin wherever we are and the
thought of the trace ... has already taught us that it was impossible to justify
a point of departure absolutely. *Wherever we are*: in a text where we already
believe ourselves to be' (Derrida, 1976, p. 162). It is possible to trace a series of
substitutions forever. For Derrida there is no master word, no ultimate foundation
of meaning that must end the series. I begin within texts signed 'Jacques Derrida'
where I believe it fruitful for educators to begin. I begin with a discussion
of 'différance' and the ethical, political, and institutional nature of Derrida's
thought.

Différance and the Place of the Ethical, Political, and Institutional in Derrida

Derrida (1982) starts his explication of différance with a description of the function of the sign:

> The sign is usually said to be put in the place of the thing itself, the present thing, 'thing' here standing equally for meaning or referent. The sign represents the present in its absence ... The sign, in this sense, is deferred presence. (p. 9)

Derrida deconstructs anything—transcendental consciousness, transcendent object (or Deity), or facts of nature—that presents itself as some kind of cosmic fixed point, eternal truth, or unalterable meaning. Dewey (1940/1991) insists, 'The eternal and immutable is the consummation of mortal man's quest for certainty' (pp. 98–99). Derrida deconstructs the quest for certainty, or what he calls 'the transcendental signified,' the belief that there is some eternal, immutable, and final reference for discourse, writing, or inquiry. Logocentrism, for Derrida, just means the immediate presence of a perfectly self-identical meaning or object; especially the immediately present object of pure knowledge. Logocentrism presumes that inquiry may complete the quest for certainty and arrive at an immediately present, self-identical object of thought or reason.

Différance indicates a double meaning in all language. First, there is 'difference;' the sign is different from the signified. Second, there is 'deferred presence.' For structuralist thinkers any system of signs (e.g. a theory, a text, a narrative) eventually terminates either in some master word in the system or in some 'transcendental signified,' that is, something outside the symbolic system to which all the symbols individually or in grammatical combination refer (see Derrida, 1976, p. 158). The transcendental signified terminates the play of signs because it is, supposedly, the presence of the indubitable self-identical thing, the referent. Derrida denies the existence of the transcendental signified, thereby challenging Western metaphysics. Derrida (1978), though, does understand the desire to escape the anxiety of uncertainty:

> The concept of centered structure is in fact the concept of a play based on a fundamental ground, a play constituted on the basis of a fundamental immobility and a reassuring certitude, which itself is beyond the reach of play. And on the basis of the certitude anxiety can be mastered ... a history—whose origin may always be reawakened or whose end may always be anticipated in the form of presence. (p. 279)

The promise is false, but the human need is real.

Against those who condemn him as merely de\structive, Derrida argues, 'Deconstruction certainly entails a moment of affirmation. Indeed, I cannot conceive of a radical critique which would not be ultimately motivated by some sort of affirmation, acknowledged or not. Deconstruction always presupposes affirmation' (see Kearney, 1984, p. 118). Derrida is quite clear about what he wants to affirm; deconstruction, for him, is 'an openness towards the other' (see Kearney, 1984,

p. 124). Deconstruction problematizes because it constantly points away from itself toward absence and otherness. It welcomes in advance the excluded 'other.' Derrida states deconstruction's affirmation thus:

> I mean that deconstruction is, in itself, a positive response to an alterity which necessarily calls, summons or motivates it. Deconstruction is therefore vocation—a response to a call. The other, as the other than self, the other that opposes self-identity ... The other precedes philosophy and necessarily invokes and provokes the subject before any genuine questioning can begin. It is in this rapport with the other that affirmation expresses itself. (in Kearney, 1995, p. 168)

Deconstruction urges recognition and respect for what is different, left out, or queer. It is this positive response to the 'other,' to those persons and situations different from the 'norm' that, in writing my paper, I want most to urge educators to consider. What is called for is not the arrogance of institutionalized knowledge with its rigid standards, categories, and identities, but acknowledgement, respect, and, perhaps, recognition.

There is no ultimate beginning or ending in Derrida's world; nor is there a bottom (or top) to Being. Derrida (1978) rejects the metaphysics of invariable presence and its retinue:

> The entire history of the concept of structure ... must be thought of as a series of substitutions of center for center, as a linked chain of determinations of the center ... It could be shown that all names related to fundamentals, to principles, or to the center have always designated an invariable presence—*eidos*, *arche*, *telos*, *energeia*, *ousia* (essence, existence, substance, subject) ... (pp. 279–280)

Eidos refers to something's characteristic form, or essence. *Arche* refers to ultimate origin, foundation, or first principle. *Energeia* is the functioning of a capacity or potential to achieve its fulfillment and actualization. It conjoins with *entelecheia*; that is, the capacity or force to achieve its perfect self-actualization. For instance, a properly functioning acorn will become a giant oak. *Telos* refers to completion, end, or purpose; it also connects with *entelecheia*. *Ousia* refers to ultimate substance or subject.

In an essay on 'Metaphysics and Essence', Derrida (1978) urges,

> *Respect* for the other *as what it is*: other. Without this acknowledgment, which is not a knowledge, or let us say without this 'letting-be' of an existent (Other) as something existing outside me in the essence of what it is (first in its alterity), no ethics would be possible. ... The 'letting-be' concerns all possible forms of the existent and even those which, by essence, cannot be transformed into 'objects of comprehension. (p. 138)

This is ontological respect and openness to what one does not understand. Education is an ethical practice and ethical relations begin in respect for the particular, even if unknowable, being of other beings. Logocentrism drives out difference; it

reduces everything to the essences, categories, and norms of the knower. Deconstruction exposes an ethics of acknowledgement. It opens a site for the consideration of the implications of scientific knowledge as a primary practice of ethical
knowing.

Modernity assumes progress automatically occurs if we can master nature. In the
social sciences, this means mastering human nature. The tool of mastery is Reason.
As an abstract noun reason tends to be totalizing; it tends to deny, repress, and
violate 'otherness,' difference, and uniqueness as deviations from the norm. Derrida challenges all norms by raising critical concerns about what it is that structures
these. What is it that structures meanings, practices, 'laws' that promise mastery?
His work opens questions about *why* certain practices become intelligible, valued,
deemed as traditions, while other practices become impossible, denigrated, or
unimaginable as norm\al. Unlike claims to detached, dispassionate, and neutral
rationality resting on indubitable metaphysical or epistemological foundations,
Derrida (1981) declares, 'Deconstruction ... is not *neutral*. It *intervenes*' (p. 93). It
intervenes, for instance, to deconstruct the master words used by masters of political domination to exclude participation in the political process by 'others' different
from them. This domination is all too easily translated into educational standards.
Deconstruction challenges the logocentric construction of (for example, white male)
identity as exclusively 'normal.' For his part, Dewey (1930/1984) decried 'The
efforts of those engaged in what is euphemistically called a science of education
aimed at setting so-called norms' (p. 132).

Deconstruction shakes the foundations of oppression. It is a philosophy of
connection/disconnection and inclusion/exclusion. It militates against fixed borders
and hierarchies, and we may use it to deconstruct oppressive social, political, and
institutional constructions. That is the way I approach the deconstructive
texts written under the name 'Derrida.' I will look long and hard at Derrida's
'The Laws of Reflection: Nelson Mandela, In Admiration' as a testimonial to
Derrida's (and Mandela's) deconstruction of an oppressive system of laws, an
illegal legal code. I believe Derrida's efforts in this essay both reflect his political
response to apartheid and reveal the political responsibility of his deconstructive
practices.

Mandela and the Deconstructive Laws of Reflection

Derrida has recognized that the currently available codes for taking any political
stance are not at all adequate to radical deconstruction. The impression that deconstruction is apolitical only prevails, he claims, 'because all our political codes and
terminologies still remain fundamentally metaphysical, regardless of whether they
originate from the right or the left' (see Kearney, 1984, pp. 107–126). Thus, he is
obliged to address any political theory or discussion of politics obliquely through
the posing of questions of singularity, universality, alterity, and difference. He must
also address such related topics as the ethics of relating and responding. This is the
strategy in his essay 'The Laws of Reflection: Nelson Mandela, In Admiration.' In
this essay, Derrida produces a reading of the 'Law' that he argues is reflected in a

singular person and the proper name, Nelson Mandela. It is a structure of 'Law' that Mandela, in all his particularity, opens, calls forth to transgress the determined historicity of the law as Western law. Mandela in his specificity constitutes for Derrida a gathering in action of singular traits, an apparatus of reflection that gives birth to 'the law itself, the law above other laws', 'a law beyond legality' (Derrida, 1987, pp. 11, 42). It is instantiated in his name, in his reflection upon the law, and in his reflection of it (pp. 15, 34). This is no routine exercise, for Derrida is not proclaiming or acclaiming Mandela a great man. He is paying homage, admiring him for his interrogation of the *meaning* of the law, interrogation of its origin, its aims, and its limits. Derrida shows Mandela as a figure inquiring after the grounding of the ground itself.

'Mandela', his name, is inscribed within a *common* geo-political history, tradition, and problematics. As a human being, his vocation is that of a 'man of the law' and as such he both reflects it and reflects upon it in the living of his life (Derrida, 1987, p. 26). Mandela reflects the law, but not in a simple speculative reversal because the law in South Africa has been usurped, represented by an oppressive white minority. His becomes the name of the 'Law' by the laws of reflection. They work this way. In struggling against apartheid, Mandela inspires admiration by the admiration *he feels* for the logic of the law. This admiration that demonstrates for something that by its very nature tends toward universality, generality, makes him, a singular person, admirable to his friends and to his enemies alike. Without reducing différance (in this case, his own particularity), Mandela forces 'difference,' a multiple mirroring involving the 'Law,' of which he is clearly within, and the law, which he is clearly outside.

Derrida's text as well as its subject produces a gathering of a multitude of non-symmetrical and non-speculative reflections that cannot refer or represent any totality nor create any unity or synthesis. The hypothesis in Derrida's (1987) words is that Mandela 'becomes admirable for having, with all his force, admired, and for having made a force of his admiration, a combative, untreatable, and irreducible power' (p. 15). Derrida performs this movement of reflections outside a logic of exclusive either/ors, thereby freeing the idea of difference from normative connotations. In thinking difference differently, he demonstrates a distinction between the conceptualizable difference of common sense (different from the norm) and a difference that is not brought back into the order of the same. (Mandela, *both* a man of the law *and* a man outside it). Difference here is neither an identity nor a difference between identities. The figure of Mandela deconstructs Western moral law and its basis in the logical law of identity. Mandela's Law makes its production possible by transversal of responsibility to a questioning, to the interrogative demand for a *just* structure of law. He, his name, his life irrevocably moves the discourse of politics to its ethical relation among human beings.

In this essay and others, Derrida refuses Habermas's claim, for example, that there exists a necessary link between universalism, rationalism, and modern democracy. Yet, he is strongly committed to the democratic project. He shows Mandela as a figure reflecting the lack of availability of an Archimedean point—such as Reason—that could guarantee the possibility of a mode of argumentation that would have transcended its particular conditions of enunciation. No rational grounding secures the institution of apartheid. He shows the distinction between the public man and the private man, important as it is for democratic politics, is not one of essence. Mandela's life problematizes that differentiation, reflects it as an unstable frontier constantly trespassed, with personal autonomy investing public aims, and the private as political.

The 'Laws of Reflection' elaborate a non-foundationalist thinking about democracy and I believe present a convincing case for the importance of deconstruction for politics and ethics. The radical democratic principles Mandela forces by the mobilization of passions and sentiments are only defensible in a situated contextualist manner, as being constitutive of his form of life. Derrida argues that he expresses democratic values, not by appealing to some neutral ground to some transcendental rationalist argument based on politically neutral premises, or by seeing the individual as prior to society, as abstracted from social and power relations, language, and culture. His name consists in the legitimization of conflict, keeping democratic hope alive by the refusal to eliminate it through the imposition of an authoritarian South African structure of law.

Derrida attends to the *excess* within the closure of the law by his homage to Mandela. He complicates the play of reflexivity of the code of politics in which the two concepts of 'original' and 'image' mirror each other, intensifying the slippage between 'original' and copy, between the thing and its disguise. His writing reminds us of the chain of significations in which the word 'law' is caught. He writes of Mandela:

> As a lawyer worthy of that name, he sets himself *against the code in the code*, reflects the code, but making visible thereby just what the code in action rendered unreadable ... His reflection ... does not re-produce, it produces the visible. This production of light is justice—moral or political. (p. 34)

I believe good education involves careful reflection on the moral, political and scientific codes that control its construction. This means the stories education tells itself must become interested in the archaeology of its own construction, the sedimentary grounds of its own authority. Educators encountering the 'texts' of schooling and culture must, like Mandela, move to acknowledge both the structure of the narration of the stories and what it is that structures its modes of intelligibility. The categories I use to describe ourselves and others, the meaning of our methods and aims, the maze of dualisms in which I have explained our intentions and our tools to ourselves become sites of contention.

Derrida, Dewey and the Double Bind of Postmodern Criticism

The neo-pragmatist Richard Bernstein (1992) admires Derrida's philosophy of deconstruction, particularly its openness to differences and attention to the violence wrought by exclusionary laws, norms, and standards. Although he sees deconstruction as a powerful tool for critiquing exclusive social, political and (I add) educational, practices, Bernstein thinks such radical openness finds it difficult to take strong positions in ethical, political, or institutional struggles. He believes, rightly, there is no ethics or politics possible without taking some, at least temporary, position. What Bernstein calls 'the double bind' is that Derrida wants to ameliorate the violence of Western thought by challenging logocentrism and the metaphysics of presence without falling into nihilistic relativism. Derrida recognizes the problem:

> But the difficulty is to gesture in opposite directions at the same time: on the one hand to preserve a distance and suspicion with regard to the official political codes governing reality; on the other, to intervene here and now in a practical and engaged manner whenever the necessity arises. … I try where I can to act politically while recognizing that such action remains incommensurate with my intellectual project of deconstruction. (in Kearney, 1984, p. 120)

Derrida often expresses worry about responsibility even as he authors situated, contextualized texts such as 'The Laws of Reflection.'

'Metaphysically,' writes Derrida (1978), 'the best liberation from violence is a certain putting into question, which makes the search for an *archia* tremble' (p. 141). Dewey's philosophy of reconstruction liberates us from ethical violence by including the 'other' in the same way as Derrida's deconstruction; that is, by making the metaphysics of presence tremble. He does so in ways that do not lead into Derrida's 'double bind.'

Dewey's Copernican Revolution: Decentering the metaphysics of presence

Dewey (1929/1984) intends to foment revolution, and that involves destruction, if not deconstruction; consider:

> Neither self nor world, neither soul nor nature (in the sense of something isolated and finished in its isolation) is the centre, any more than either earth or sun is the absolute centre of a single universal and necessary frame of reference. There is a moving whole of interacting parts; a centre emerges wherever there is effort to change them in a particular direction. (p. 232)

Dewey's emphasis is always on reconstruction rather than deconstruction.

Ralph Sleeper (1986) remarks that Dewey clearly distinguished 'the theory of inquiry and the theory of existence, as well as the theory of language that links them' (p. 6). 'The subject-matter of metaphysics,' notes Sleeper, 'is existence' (p. 111). The subject matter of logic is essences and identities. Dewey (1925/1981) clearly stated that 'there is a natural bridge that joins the gap between existence and essence; namely communication, language, discourse' (p. 133). Here is how Dewey describes the relation between existence and essence:

> Essence … is but a pronounced instance of [linguistic] meaning; to be partial, and to assign *a* meaning to a thing as *the* meaning is but to evince

> human subjection to bias ... Essence is never existence, and yet it is the
> essence, the distilled import of existence ... its intellectual voucher.' (p. 144)

Jean-Paul Sartre thought existence preceded essence only for human beings. For
Dewey, the distinction includes all being, although only beings capable of language
and logic (inquiry into inquiry) could bridge it, and know it. Dewey transfers the
functions normally associated with the metaphysics of presence to inquiry. For him,
the existential task is to create a cosmos from chaos by guiding indeterminate events
in new directions that promote prosperity. Directing the course of events is the
office of inquiry.

In 'The Influence of Darwinism on Philosophy,' Dewey (1909/1977) declares:

> The conception that had reigned in the philosophy of nature and
> knowledge for two thousand years ... rested on the assumption of the
> superiority of the fixed and final ... In laying hands upon the sacred ark of
> absolute permanency, in treating forms that had been regarded as types
> of fixity and perfection as originating and passing away, the *Origin
> of Species* introduced a mode of thinking that in the end was bound to
> transform the logic of knowledge, and hence the treatment of morals,
> politics and religion. (p. 3)

Dewey might well have added metaphysics. Traditional metaphysics places ultimate
ontology beyond time, contingency, and change. Dewey converts the primary subject matter of ontological metaphysics (*eidos*) into the subject matter of inquiry.
Essence is a product of inquiry and not an antecedent existence into whose immediate presence it is the task of inquiry to conduct us.

A species is the ultimate ontological subject of evolutionary theory. Dewey did
for essences what Darwin did for species. Dewey declares, 'The conception of
εἶδος, species, a fixed form and final cause, was the central principle of knowledge
as well as of nature. Upon it rested the logic of science' (p. 6). After Darwin,
Dewey (1920/1982) insists, 'natural science is forced by its own development to
abandon the assumption of fixity and to recognize that what for it is actually
"universal" is *process*' (p. 260). A species is an *eidos*. Like Derrida, Dewey (1909/
1977) recognizes the determination of *eidos* by *telos* when he states that 'the classic
notion of species carried with it the idea of purpose' (p. 8).

Estimates are that 99 per cent of all species that have ever existed are now
extinct.[2] Dewey realizes that what holds for biological essences also holds for
logical essences. Dewey (1925/1981) insists that 'even the solid earth mountains,
the emblems of constancy, appear and disappear like the clouds ... A thing may
endure *secula seculorum* and yet not be everlasting; it will crumble before the
gnawing tooth of time, as it exceeds a certain measure. Every existence is an event'
(p. 63). Dewey's reconstruction of *eidos* renders it not only completely temporal
and contingent, it also removes it from the domain of metaphysics.

Existence for Dewey is an event. There is nothing fixed and final in a Darwinian
universe. In Dewey's philosophy, existence or 'nature is viewed as consisting of events
rather than substances, it is characterized by *histories* ... Consequently, it is natural

for genuine initiations and consummations to occur in experience' (Dewey, 1925/ 1981, pp. 5–6). For him, existence, the subject matter of metaphysics, is events; it is about processes, not ultimate substances (*ousia*). Dewey's Darwinian intuition is that everything, existences, and their distilled import, essences, is in flux, everything changes; whatever is constructed will someday be either intellectually deconstructed or physically destroyed.

Dewey probably derived his thinking about essences from William James who rejects any notion of permanent fixed essence; for him there is only practical purposes. James (1890/1950) insists:

> the only meaning of essence is teleological, and that classification and conception
> *are purely teleological weapons of the mind.* The essence of a thing is that one
> of its properties which is so *important for my interests* that in comparison
> with it I may neglect the rest. (p. 335)

Questioning the purposes for which they were initially constructed can deconstruct any scheme of essences. Reinterpreting the purpose quickly deconstructs a pragmatic classification or concept. There is a *telos* to pragmatic essences, but it is practical, temporal, and contingent, not metaphysical, atemporal, and necessary.

Strangely, James continues to comprehend necessity and causation as metaphysical. Dewey does for necessity and causation what James did for essences. Sleeper (1986): 'The [scientific] explanation has not so much been "discovered" as "produced" by the process of inquiry. The character of "necessity," therefore, is "purely teleological" and contingent' (p. 37). For Dewey (1893/1971), both contingency and necessity are moments in the continuous movement of inquiry:

> Contingent and necessary are thus the correlative aspects of one and the
> same fact ... Contingency referring to the separation of means from end
> ... necessity being the reference of means to an end which has still to be
> got. Necessary means needed; contingency means no longer required—
> because already enjoyed. (p. 29)

Dewey understands necessity 'only with reference to the development of judgment, not with reference to objective things or events' (p. 19). Following James's treatment of essences, Dewey comprehends necessity as a logical and not an ontological concept. Necessary laws are dependent on the inquirer's purposes and, therefore, are endlessly subject to deconstruction. Dewey's view of necessity helps undermine the sense of *energeia* and *entelecheia* found in the metaphysics of presence.

Dewey includes causation in his analysis of necessity: 'We call it "means and ends" when we set up a result to be reached in the future ... we call it "cause and effect" when the "result" is given and the search for means is a regressive one' (p. 36). Again he affirms 'the supreme importance of our practical interests' (p. 36). As with formal essences (*eidos*) and necessity (part of the *arche*), Dewey assimilates causation (*energeia*, *entelecheia*, or *telos*) to logic, not metaphysics. Dewey's strategy is one of draining the swamp of Western metaphysics into the basin of logic.

In the following passage, Dewey (1909/1977) drains off a great deal: 'Philosophy forswears inquiry after absolute origins and absolute finalities in order to explore specific values and the specific conditions that generate them' (p. 10). There is no ultimate cosmic beginning (*arche*) or ending (*telos*) in Dewey's naturalistic Darwinian world any more than there is in Derrida's deconstructive one. Origins and teleology, including *entelecheia*, or *eidos*, are only comprehensible within the context of purposeful logical inquiry, not metaphysics.

Dewey effectively rejects the quest for the transcendental signified:

> Once admit that the sole verifiable or fruitful object of knowledge is the particular set of changes that generate the object of study, together with the consequences that then flow from it, and no intelligible question can be asked about what, by assumption, lies outside. (p. 11)

Objects of knowledge, essences, necessity, causation, etc., do not exist outside the confines of inquiry. This is 'the direction of the transformation in philosophy to be wrought by the Darwinian genetic and experimental logic' (p. 13). Dewey's naturalism refuses to extend itself beyond the contingent products of disciplined inquiry conducted for finite human purposes.

As a pragmatist, Dewey emphasizes the importance of the relatively stable and fixed more so than Derrida. This permits him to take critical positions more readily. Still, every construction is contingent in a Darwinian universe; hence, every construction is subject to deconstruction and reconstruction. In this process, Dewey puts the accent on the constructive and reconstructive phase more than the deconstructive. Dewey's neo-Darwinism imparts urgency to his philosophy of reconstruction that is missing from Derrida's deconstruction. This is the way out of Derrida's 'double bind' and a more responsible attitude to take.

Metaphysics, Criticism, and Context: Finding temporary positions for creative criticism

Bernstein (1992) complains that criticism of all kinds has been 'drawn into a grand Either/Or: either there is a rational grounding of the norms of critique or the conviction that there is such a rational grounding is itself a self-deceptive illusion' (p. 8). Most educational thought falls into such grand either/ors. Instead of assuming either one or the other opinion must be the right one, Bernstein suggests an alternative. He believes that critique goes on forever, the final meaning not only of the critiqued object, but also of critique itself, is forever deferred. Bernstein (1992) concludes, 'I do not think we can any longer responsibly claim that there is or can be a final reconciliation in which all difference, "otherness," opposition and contradiction are reconciled' (p. 8).

Bernstein suggests we think of criticism as constituted by a 'logic' that avoids conceptual universals or the either/or. He advocates a both/and 'logic' rather than the logocentrism of perfect identity. That is why Bernstein (1992) admires the way 'Derrida deconstructs the Either/Or itself' (p. 184). Nonetheless, Bernstein remains concerned with the question: '*how can we "warrant" ... the ethical-political "positions" we do take?* This is *the* question that Derrida never satisfactorily answers ... What are we to do after we realize that all *archia* tremble?' (p. 191). Dewey responds to these questions better than Derrida, although the difference is more one of emphasis and attitude than fundamental philosophical disagreement. Both emphasize the cyclic relation between criticism and creativity. In the critical/creative cycle of construction–deconstruction–reconstruction, Derrida tends to emphasize deconstruction; whereas Dewey accents reconstruction.

Those who do not grasp the critical importance of creative play often deride Derrida for his lack of seriousness. Dewey wants only to constrain the field of play in responsible ways. Dewey (1930/1984) declares:

> Ideals express possibilities; but they are genuine ideals only in so far as they are possibilities of what is now moving. Imagination can set them free from their encumbrances and project them as a guide in attention to what now exists. But, save as they are related to actualities, they are pictures in a dream. (p. 112)

For Dewey, concrete, embodied lived situations constrain possibility in ways that Derrida seems to ignore. The task of inquiry, including educational inquiry, is to connect the ideal with the actual to transform the present situation. Ideas, hypotheses, etc. mediate between the undesirable actuality and the ideal possibility.

One may enjoy free imaginative play when one is at leisure, safe and secure. Often we first glimpse our most desperate desires as a dream or fantasy. Dreams, though, can be dangerous, even deadly, in a world where 99 per cent of species that have ever existed are now extinct. Derrida is right to emphasize play; it is a delight and necessary for survival. Still, excessive deconstruction can lead to destruction in a Darwinian world. Dewey seems to understand this threat better than Derrida; that is why he places greater emphasis on reconstruction instead of deconstruction. Dewey always firmly situates freedom; that is why he chooses to emphasize real possibility grounded in the current actual state of concrete affairs, rather than abstract possibility. The horizon separating real possibilities from those too distant to actualize is difficult to discern for even the most experienced captain of the ship of responsible critique. Sailing the ship of continuous critique means constantly searching the open horizon for material to reconstruct the vessel while remaining afloat.

Consequences for Education

Dewey and Derrida both make the metaphysics of presence tremble. The consequence is a cultural catachresis that extends to the site of cultural reproduction—education. If there are no fixed essences, then there is no fixed human essence. Without a fixed essence (*eidos*), education has no ultimate, immutable, and eternal fixed *telos* that represents the perfection (*entelecheia*) of the process of education. There is no *arche* of timeless immutable foundations of education. Children are not substances (*ousia*) with the latent potential to actualize (*energeia*) their essence any more than acorns alone have the latent potential to actualize their essence as a giant oak tree. What children become depends on the transactions they enter. Choosing these wisely, we may survive and thrive in an ever-changing Darwinian world. Learning to makes such choices is an educational task. So, what is the aim of education? Dewey's (1916/1980) answer is: 'Since growth is the characteristic of life, education is all one with growing; it has no end beyond itself' (p. 58). The aim of education is growth just as the meaning of life for an existentialist like Dewey is to make more meaning.

Separating metaphysical existence from logical essence clears up a great deal of existential ambiguity. Draining the swamp of metaphysics into the logic of inquiry allows us to construct enduring essences (*eidos*), temporary telos (*telos*), flying perfection (*entelecheia*), relatively stable foundations (*arche*—even the earth's tectonic plates move), and sufficient substance (*ousia*) to serve the *functions* of inquiry without the promise of completing the quest for certainty. Each may function as a transient 'centre,' a temporary position, for efforts to redirect existence. I believe that Derrida, in fact, does much the same thing. Serge Doubrovsky asks Derrida, 'You always speak of a *non-center*. How can you, within your own perspective, explain or at least understand what a perception is? For a perception is precisely the manner in which the world appears *centered* to me' (cited in Macksey and Donato, 1970, p. 271). Derrida's reply is revealing:

> First of all, I didn't say that there was no center, that we could get along without the center. I believe that the center is a function, not a being—a reality, but a function. And this function is absolutely indispensable. The subject is absolutely indispensable. I don't destroy the subject; I situate it.
> (cited in Macksey and Donato, 1970, p. 271)

I believe that, for Derrida as for Dewey, centers arise whenever there is an effort to redirect the course of events, but these centers are merely functions (or subfunctions) within a larger context. Subjects persist, but they become situated and contingent functions that we cannot disconnect from their context. Nelson Mandela is an example of such a subject who functions in ways that require us to interrogate the *meaning* of the law, its origin, its aims, and its limits. Mandela engages in an inquiry in which he reflects and reflects upon the logic of the law. In so doing, I believe he carries out a Deweyan inquiry in which essences, telos, perfections, foundations, and substances are not only subject to deconstruction, but serve the *functions* of inquiry without the promise of completion. An insightful student of Derrida such as Peter Trifonas (2000) can write:

> Deconstruction, however, if we are to believe Derrida, *does not, cannot, nor does it wish to exact the death of logocentrism*, to eliminate it, despite troubling the epistemic validity of a phonological prototype of signification that linearises the relation of *signans* and *signatum*. (p. 274)

Derrida knows we cannot live without relative centers and all that goes with them, nor can we complete the quest for certainty. What we can do is learn to live in a radically contingent and infinitely pluralistic universe. On that, both Derrida and Dewey are in profound agreement.

What can we say about Nelson Mandela besides his ability to engage in profound inquiry? For one thing, he is precisely the type of transient center of cultural deconstruction and reconstruction that emerges wherever there is effort to change events in a particular direction. He is singular, particular and, from the perspective of colonialism, a radical alterity. He would have to be such an 'other' to bring about profound social change. As Dewey (1925/1981) states, 'mind in an individualized mode has occasionally some constructive operation. Every invention, every improvement in art ... has its genesis in observation and ingenuity of a particular innovator' (p. 164). Mandela is also a source of connection/disconnection that simultaneously breaks codes and enacts them. He is a responsible source of *both* deconstruction *and* reconstruction, able to construct temporary positions that overcome 'the double bind' of alleviating violence without falling into nihilism. There is a telos to his action, but no timeless and unalterable essence of justice for him to enact. For Dewey, and Derrida, there are no cosmic purposes guaranteeing progress. Dewey (1922/1983) states:

> There is something pitifully juvenile in the idea that 'evolution,' progress, means a definite sum of accomplishment which will forever stay done, and which by an exact amount lessens the amount still to be done, disposing once and for all of just so many perplexities and advancing us just so far on our road to a final stable and unperplexed goal. (p. 197)

We can do our best without any cosmic backup story guaranteeing success. That is part of maturity and the attitude of the meliorist in contrast to the optimist. Dewey (1920/1982) writes:

> Meliorism is the belief that the specific conditions which exist at one moment, be they comparatively bad or comparatively good, in any event may be bettered. (pp. 181–182)

I believe Mandela is a meliorist who may or may not believe in progress.

Mandela is an excellent particular example of the kind of creative, deconstructive, and melioristic individual that education should strive to create. I believe such paradoxical characters, schooled in the 'logic' of both, are ideal personalities for dealing with the tensions of the double bind. Derrida and Dewey pose a tremendous challenge to educators, and for that we should admire them.

Acknowledgements

I thank Larry Hickman and Patti Lather for their helpful comments. I especially thank Mary Leach for allowing me to use her words in this paper, but in a context with which she does not fully agree. This paper draws extensively from Garrison and Leach (2001). Anyone who consults that text will know my debt to Mary, and our creative, and caring, differences.

Notes

1. See Derrida, 1996, p. 78.
2. See Parker, 1992, pp. 57–58.

References

Bernstein, R. (1992) *The New Constellation* (Cambridge, MA, MIT Press).
Derrida, J. (1976) *Of Grammatology*, trans. G. C. Spivak (Baltimore, Johns Hopkins Press).
Derrida, J. (1978) *Writing and Difference*, trans. A. Bass (Chicago, University of Chicago Press).
Derrida, J. (1981) *Positions*, trans. A. Bass (Chicago, University of Chicago Press).
Derrida, J. (1982) *Margins of Philosophy*, trans. A. Bass (Chicago, University of Chicago Press).
Derrida, J. (1987) The Laws of Reflection: Nelson Mandela, in: J. Derrida & M. Tlili (eds), *Admiration, for Nelson Mandela* (New York, Seaver Books, Henry Holt and Company).
Derrida, (1996) Remarks on Deconstruction and Pragmatism, in: C. Mouffe (ed.), *Deconstruction and Pragmatism* (London, Routledge), pp. 77–88.
Dewey, J. (1893/1971) The Superstition of Necessity, in: J. A. Boydston (ed.), *John Dewey: The early works*, vol. 4 (Carbondale, Southern Illinois University Press), pp. 19–36.
Dewey, J. (1909/1977) The Influence of Darwinism on Philosophy, in: J. A. Boydston (ed.), *John Dewey: The middle works*, vol. 4 (Carbondale, Southern Illinois University Press), pp. 3–14.
Dewey, J. (1916/1980) Democracy and Education, in: J. A. Boydston (ed.), *John Dewey: The middle works*, vol. 9 (Carbondale, Southern Illinois University Press).
Dewey, J. (1920/1982) Reconstruction in Philosophy, in: J. A. Boydston (ed.), *John Dewey: The middle works*, vol. 12 (Carbondale, Southern Illinois University Press).
Dewey, J. (1922/1983) Human Nature and Conduct, in: J. A. Boydston (ed.), *John Dewey: The middle works*, vol. 14 (Carbondale, Southern Illinois University Press).
Dewey, J. (1925/1981) Experience and Nature, in: J. A. Boydston (ed.), *John Dewey: The later works*, vol. 1 (Carbondale, Southern Illinois University Press).
Dewey, J. (1929/1984) The Quest for Certainty, in: J. A. Boydston (ed.), *John Dewey: The later works*, vol. 4 (Carbondale, Southern Illinois University Press).
Dewey, J. (1930/1984) From Absolutism to Experimentalism, in: J. A. Boydston (ed.), *John Dewey: The later works*, vol. 5 (Carbondale, Southern Illinois University Press).
Dewey, J. (1940/1991) Time and Individuality, in: J. A. Boydston (ed.), *John Dewey: The later works*, vol. 14 (Carbondale, Southern Illinois University Press), pp. 98–114.
Garrison, J. & Leach, M. (2001) Dewey after Derrida, in: V. Richardson (ed.), *Handbook of Research on Teaching*, 4th edn (Washington, DC, American Educational Research Association).
James, W. (1890/1950) *The Principles of Psychology*, vol. 2 (New York, Dover Publications, Inc.), pp. 69–81.
Kamuf, P. (ed.) (1991) Letter to a Japanese Friend, *A Derrida Reader* (New York, Columbia University Press).
Kearney, R. (ed.) (1984) Deconstruction and the Other, in: *Dialogues with Contemporary Continental Thinkers* (Manchester, Manchester University Press).
Kearney, R. (ed.) (1995) Jacques Derrida: Deconstruction and the other, in: *States of Mind: Dialogues with contemporary thinkers* (New York, New York University Press).
Macksey, R. & Donato, E. (1970) *The Languages of Criticism and the Sciences of Man: The structuralist controversy* (Baltimore: Johns Hopkins Press).
Parker, S. P. (ed.) (1992) *McGraw-Hill Encyclopedia of Science & Technology*, vol. 6 (7th edn, New York, McGraw-Hill), pp. 570–572.
Sleeper, R. (1986) *The Necessity of Pragmatism* (New Haven, Yale University Press).
Trifonas, P. (2000) Jacques Derrida as a Philosopher of Education, *Educational Philosophy and Theory*, 32:3, pp. 271–281.

Index